INSTANT POT COOKBOOK

Karen Benett

Copyright © 2017

Symbol Press

All Rights Reserved

All rights reserved. No part of this book may be reproduced or transmitted in any form or by any means, electronic or mechanical, including photocopying, recording or by any information storage and retrieval system, without written permission from the publisher, except for the inclusion of brief quotations in a review.

Warning-Disclaimer

The purpose of this book is to educate and entertain. The author or publisher does not guarantee that anyone following the techniques, suggestions, tips, ideas, or strategies will become successful. The author and publisher shall have neither liability or responsibility to anyone with respect to any loss or damage caused, or alleged to be caused, directly or indirectly by the information contained in this book.

CONTENTS

INTRODUCTION 7

   Before You Buy that Instant Pot: Exploring the Science of Pressure Cooking 8

   Top 3 Reasons to Use the Instant Pot Rather than Stovetop 12

   Instant Pot Cooking Time Chart .. 14

VEGETABLES & SIDE DISHES .. 20

   1. Potato and Wheat Berry Breakfast 21

   2. Egg and Spinach Cup Custards 22

   3. Cauliflower and Anchovy Salad 23

   4. Broccoli and Pineapple Salad 24

   5. Greek-Style Wheat Berries 25

   6. Summer Quinoa Salad 26

   7. Cannellini Salad with Peppers and Carrots 27

   8. Tender Vegetables with Walnuts 28

   9. Creamy Vegetable Soup 29

   10. Pureed Cauliflower Soup with Cheese 30

   11. Vegetarian Mushroom Stew ... 31

   12. Summer Tomato-Potato Soup 32

   13. Red Cabbage with Apples 33

   14. Mediterranean Tomato Risotto 34

   15. Porcini Mushroom Curry 35

POULTRY 36

   16. Seasoned Chicken with Cheese . 37

   17. Easiest Chicken Risotto 38

   18. Chicken and Barley Soup with Garbanzo Beans 39

   19. Mom's Chicken Soup 40

   20. Chicken and Yogurt Curry 41

   21. Summer Chicken Chili 42

   22. Tender Garlicky Chicken 43

   23. Hot Dinner Stew 44

   24. Red Curry Chicken Thighs ... 45

   25. Pasta with Chicken and Raisins 46

   26. Festive Chicken with Beans .. 47

   27. Chicken in Herbed Lemon Sauce 48

   28. Family Baked Chicken 49

   29. Crispy Chicken Wings with Herbed Sauce 50

   30. Creamed Chicken with Yogurt Sauce 51

   31. Curried Turkey Soup 52

   32. Balsamic Turkey Wings 53

   33. Turkey and Bean Chili 54

   34. Sausage and Garbanzo Bean Stew 55

   35. Ground Turkey Stew with Spinach 56

PORK 57

36. Pork Sausage Gravy 58
37. Savory Ham Bread Pudding.. 59
38. Barbeque Pork Roast 60
39. Soft Peppery Carnitas 61
40. Sunday Pork and Mushroom Treat 62
41. Cabbage with Barley and Meat 63
42. Pork Sausage with Tomato and Corn 64
43. Juicy BBQ Pork 65
44. Pork and Lotus Root Soup 66
45. Root Vegetable Soup with Pork Ribs 67
46. Coconut Pork Curry 68
47. Slow Cooker Holiday Meatloaf 69
48. Juicy Pork Belly 70
49. BBQ Pork Ribs with Garden Vegetables 71
50. Festive Pot Roast 72
51. Comforting Potato and Bacon Soup 73
52. Old-Fashioned Cassoulet 74
53. Spiced Chinese Ribs 75
54. Penne with Sausage and Tomato Sauce 76
55. Spanish Chorizo and Garbanzo Beans with Escarole 77

BEEF 78

56. Country Beef Hash 79
57. Beef and Green Bean Soup ... 80
58. Soft Vegetable Pot Roast 81
59. Peasant Tomato Cabbage Rolls 82
60. Beef Brisket with Tomatillo Sauce 83
61. Short Ribs with Pearl Onions and Potatoes 84
62. Old-fashioned Rich Stew 85
63. Italian-Style Beef Soup 86
64. Traditional Beef Stroganoff 87
65. Old-Fashioned Minestrone Soup 88
66. Herby Pasta with Meat and Mushrooms 89
67. Orange Short Ribs 90
68. Pulled BBQ Beef 91
69. Herbed Mustard Roast 92
70. Spaghetti with Bacon and Beef Sauce 93
71. Hamburger Cabbage and Barley Soup 94
72. Beef and Yogurt Curry 95
73. Beef and Kale Stew with Noodles 96
74. Holiday Short Ribs 97
75. BBQ Beef Sandwiches 98

FISH & SEAFOOD 99

76. Tuna Salad with Noodles and Mozzarella 100
77. Saucy Fish Fillets with Onion 101
78. Creamy Fish Curry 102
79. Rice and Tuna Salad 103

80. Cod Fillets with
Cremini Mushrooms....................104

81. Salmon Fillets in
Mayonnaise Sauce 105

82. Sausage and
Seafood Delight 106

83. Tuna and Brown
Rice Salad....................................107

84. Tuna with Noodles
and Feta 108

85. Saucy Salmon Fillets............109

VEGAN 110

86. Homemade Pumpkin Purée...111

87. Romantic Apricot Oatmeal .. 112

88. Basic Apple Sauce................. 113

89. Morning Aromatic Congee .. 114

90. Cilantro Breakfast Quinoa .. 115

91. Potato and Porcini
Mushroom Soup........................... 116

92. Kidney Bean Salad 117

93. Easy Key Lime Quinoa 118

94. Perfect Banana
Barley Congee.............................. 119

95. Old-fashioned Savory
Rice Porridge 120

96. Nutty Oatmeal with
Dried Fruits................................. 121

97. Banana and Chia
Seed Porridge 122

98. Wheat Berry Salad
with Cranberries 123

99. Hearty Mushroom-Bean
Soup 124

100. Sunday Barley Congee 125

101. Prune and Pear
Vegan Oatmeal.............................126

102. Bean and Apple Salad 127

103. Sweet Potato Soup
with Peanut Butter......................128

104. Creamed Summer
Squash Soup 129

105. Easiest and Tastiest
Hummus Ever 130

106. Homemade
Mushroom Pâté............................ 131

107. Baby Carrots with
Goat Cheese and Almonds 132

108. Spiced Acorn
Squash Appetizer........................133

109. Warm Russet
Potato Appetizer 134

110. Steamed Lemony
Artichokes 135

111. Orange-Glazed
Chicken Wings 136

112. Rich Sausage
and Tomato Dip............................137

113. Appetizer Meatballs
in Tomato Sauce 138

114. Classic Buffalo
Chicken Wings..............................139

115. Tomato Pork Dip.................140

116. Kale and Carrot Appetizer .. 141

117. Cheesy Corn Dip 142

118. Potato Mash
with Marjoram 143

119. Herby Polenta
quares with Cheese 144

120. Delicious Fingerling
Potatoes.......................................145

121. Squash and Pineapple Treat 146

122. Cremini Mushrooms and Asparagus Appetizer 147

123. Chili Pumpkin Hummus 148

124. Maple Brussels Sprouts 149

125. Famous Lemon-Garlic Corn on the Cob 150

BEANS & GRAINS 151

126. Yummy Apple Oatmeal 152

127. Raisin-Cinnamon Rice Pudding 153

128. Date Cinnamon Bread Pudding 154

129. Nutty Bulgur and Oat Porridge 155

130. Cheese and Tabasco Grits .. 156

131. Bean and Mint Salad 157

132. Yam Barley Congee 158

133. Butter Bean Casserole 159

134. Sausage and Navy Bean Soup with Greens 160

135. Mushroom and Bean Vegetarian Soup 161

136. Creamy Breakfast Risotto with Blackberries 162

137. Polenta with Pecans and Honey 163

138. Chili Bean and Ham Bone Soup 164

139. Spiced Beans with Turkey 165

140. Berry Banana Rice Porridge 166

DESSERTS 167

141. Fresh Currant Bread Pudding 168

142. Vegan Pumpkin Cake 169

143. Pumpkin Chocolate Bundt Cake 170

144. Tropical Tapioca Pudding 171

145. Star Anise Chocolate Cake 172

146. Banana-Vanilla Rice Pudding 173

147. Cheesecake with Cranberry Topping 174

148. Rustic Apple Compote 175

149. Festive Dessert with Prunes and Pecans 176

150. Frozen Lime Cheesecake 177

INTRODUCTION

If you are considering a health-oriented and fast-paced lifestyle, an electric pressure cooker is the right kitchen tool for you. The Instant pot is a revolutionary multi-cooker that utilizes one-touch technology, high temperatures and high-pressure to cook your food in a healthy way while saving your time and money.

Choosing an electric pressure cooker doesn't mean skimping on flavor. As a matter of fact, it means reaching for the healthier and faster versions of your favorite dishes! This book will give you the guidelines to get the most out of your Instant pot.

The Instant Pot is a multifunctional programmable cooker that can do the job of an electric pressure cooker, a slow cooker, rice maker, a steamer, a sautéing pan, a warming pot, and yogurt maker. Thus, the Instant pot is given a place of honor on the kitchen countertop!

BEFORE YOU BUY THAT INSTANT POT: EXPLORING THE SCIENCE OF PRESSURE COOKING

Put it in a nutshell, the whole cooking process in the Instant pot is easy to follow. You plug it in, throw in the ingredients, seal the lid, press the desired button, and let it go. However, regardless of this simplicity, there are several things to bear in mind that can help you achieve the best results. Doubtless, you should read the manual that comes with the appliance carefully before using your Instant pot.

The Instant pot consists of an inner pot (a removable cooking pot), the lid with a gasket, the electric heating element, safety valves and temperature/pressure sensors.

The first remarkable feature of the Instant pot is a smart programming; the second one is an enhanced safety. The process is controlled by the built-in microprocessor with intelligent cooking capabilities that can be programmed to perform very complicated tasks.

The Instant Pot is capable of adjusting cooking cycle depending on the amount of the chosen food and to change pressure based on the food type.

Basically, there are four parameters such as temperature, heating intensity, duration and pressure with which this intelligent device controls the cooking process.

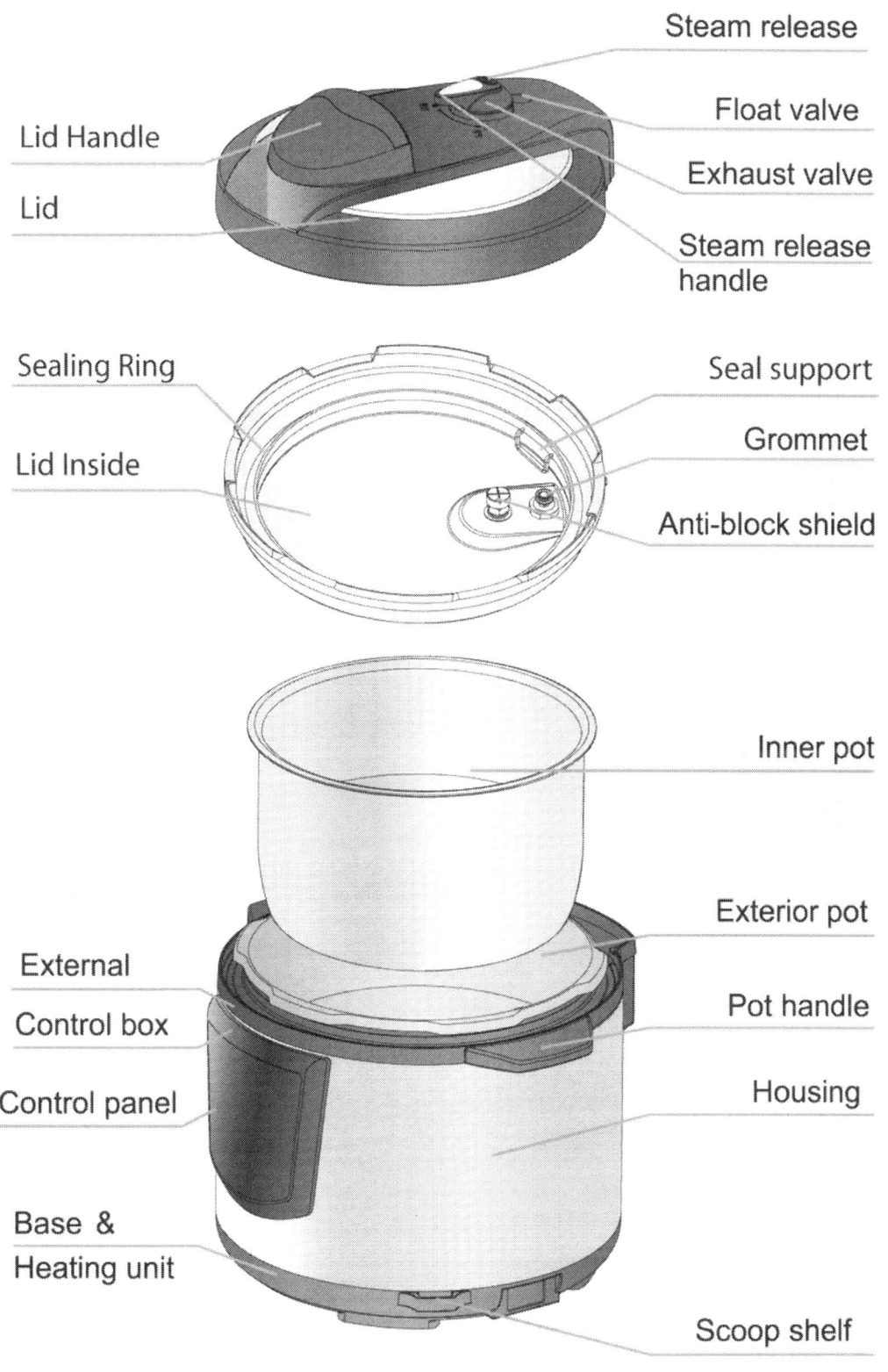

When you take a look at the control panel on your Instant pot, you can see a number of smart cooking programs:

MANUAL – the most common setting; you can easily adjust the time and temperature; in fact, this is an all-purpose button.

SAUTÉ – you can sear and brown the meat as well as to sweat your veggies without an additional cookware.

PORRIDGE – a porridge and grains are made easy with this program.

RICE – the program that is designed to boil or steam rice.

MEAT/STEW – a function specifically for cooking budget-friendly meat.

POULTRY – it can be used for cooking chicken, turkey, or duck.

SOUP – a great program designed for the best homey soups.

BEAN/CHILI – this key is for making your favorite chilies and beans.

STEAM – use a metal steam rack or steamer basket with this function.

SLOW COOK – an excellent choice for everyone who wants a meal ready when they arrive home.

MULTIGRAIN – it is the fully automated function for cooking mixed grains and wild rice quickly and effortlessly.

YOGURT – a two-step program designed for making a homemade Greek-style yogurt and regular yogurt.

KEEP WARM/CANCEL – this function is so useful: once cooking is complete, push the "Cancel" key; otherwise, the warming function is automatically activated.

Finally, we have two ways of releasing the pressure and opening the cooker:

1. **THE NATURAL PRESSURE RELEASE METHOD** – simply choose the "Cancel" button or unplug your cooker; allow it to stand until the float valve sinks and wait for about 10 minutes before releasing any remaining steam.
2. **QUICK PRESSURE RELEASE** – it's a great function to stop the pressure cooking quickly.

When it comes to cleaning and caring for your intelligent cooker, unplug it and clean the inner pot with soapy water. Clean the lid with a wet cloth and then, wipe it dry. Wipe the inside rim of the outer pot using a dry cloth.

As you get more comfortable with your Instant pot, you'll be able to adapt any traditional recipe to use with this amazing kitchen appliance. In addition, you will be able to adjust cooking times and measurements to fit your preferences. At that point, a real Instant pot adventure begins!

TOP 3 REASONS TO USE THE INSTANT POT RATHER THAN STOVETOP

A great way to boost your savings. There are a lot of ways to eat on a budget with your pressure cooker. Simply cook double the quantity of grains and beans and keep them in your fridge; buy in bulk and opt for less expensive cuts of meat because the Instant pot can tenderize any cheap cut of steak or pork and turn them into great-tasting meals. Many Instant pot recipes call for staples you already have in your kitchen like oats, beans, grains, rice, sausage, chicken thighs, pork ribs, and so forth.

Cooking doesn't have to be time-consuming. Most people don't have hours to spend cooking, especially over the week. The Instant pot is a super-sophisticated machine that saves your time while cooking the healthiest and the most flavorful dishes that otherwise would take hours to make.

For instance, it may take you over an hour to cook dry soaked beans using a traditional method of cooking; on the other hand, it will take you approximately 20 minutes to cook your beans in the Instant pot.

The Instant pot is also a clever space-saving appliance because you will be able to prepare an entire meal in just on pot. You will be able to sauté, steam, bake, cook and so forth.

Healthy "fast food". When it comes to a healthy food, it's hard to beat an electric pressure cooker. Surveys have proven that pressure cooking tends to preserve important vitamins and minerals better than frying, roasting, boiling and even steaming; nutrients actually can't escape from the sealed environment. Pressure cooking requires the minimum amount of oil and less water so that nutrients are not dissolved away by cooking liquid. A shorter cooking time, super-heated steam and automatically regulated pressure are key factors to a better and healthier cooking.

Try these outstanding recipes that combine tradition and modernity and they will make their way to your table with results that satisfy. Let's make a difference – dig into your kitchen cabinet, redefine a grandma's way of eating, explore a new generation electric pressure cooker, and turn your kitchen into a magical space! Eventually, the Instant pot will change your life forever!

INSTANT POT COOKING TIME CHART

Please note that cooking times are approximate; use them as a guideline only. These cooking times are for the medium amount of food. In order to cook a large amount of food, you should add more liquid and increase the time by 20-40%.

BEANS, LEGUMES & LENTILS	Dry, Cooking Time in Minutes	Soaked, Cooking Time in Minutes
Adzuki	20 – 25	10 – 15
Anasazi	20 – 25	10 – 15
Black beans	20 – 25	10 – 15
Black-eyed peas	20 – 25	10 – 15
Chickpeas	35 – 40	20 – 25
Cannellini beans	35 – 40	20 – 25
Gandules	20 – 25	15 – 20
Great Northern beans	25 – 30	20 – 25
Lentils, French green	15 – 20	N/A
Lentils, green and brown	15 – 20	N/A
Lentils, red and split	15 – 18	N/A
Lentils (moong dal)	15 – 18	N/A
Lima beans	20 – 25	10 – 15
Kidney beans, red	25 – 30	20 – 25
Kidney beans, white	35 – 40	20 – 25
Navy beans	25 – 30	20 – 25
Pinto beans	25 – 30	20 – 25
Peas	15 – 20	10 – 15
Soy beans	25 – 30	20 – 25

FISH & SEAFOOD	Fresh, Cooking Time in Minutes	Frozen, Cooking Time in Minutes
Crab	3 – 4	5 – 6
Fish fillet	2 – 3	3 – 4
Fish steak	3 – 4	4 – 6
Lobster	3 – 4	4 – 6
Mussels	2 – 3	4 – 5
Seafood soup or stock	6 – 7	7 – 9
Shrimp	1 – 2	2 – 3
Snapper, whole	5 – 6	7 – 10
Trout, whole	5 – 6	7 – 10

RICE & GRAINS	Water Quantity (Grain : Water ratio)	Cooking Time in Minutes
Barley, pearl	1:4	25 – 30
Congee, thick	1:4 ~ 1:5	15 – 20
Congee, thin	1:6 ~ 1:7	15 – 20
Couscous	1:2	5 – 8
Corn, dried	1:3	25 – 30
Kamut, whole	1:3	10 – 12
Millet	1:1 2/3	10 – 12
Oats, quick cooking	1:1 2/3	6
Oats, steel-cut	1:1 2/3	10
Porridge, thin	1:6 ~ 1:7	15 – 20
Quinoa, quick cooking	1:2	8
Rice, Basmati	1: 1.5	4 – 8
Rice, Brown	1: 1.25	22 – 28
Rice, Jasmine	1: 1	4 – 10
Rice, white	1: 1.5	8
Rice, wild	1:3	25 – 30
Sorghum	1:3	20 – 25
Spelt berries	1:3	15 – 20
Wheat berries	1:3	25 – 30

VEGETABLES	Fresh, Cooking Time in Minutes	Frozen, Cooking Time in Minutes
Artichokes, whole	9 – 11	11 – 13
Artichokes, hearts	4 – 5	5 – 6
Artichokes, baby	4	5 – 6
Asparagus, whole	1 – 2	2 – 3
Beans, green and yellow	1 – 2	2 – 3
Beets, small	11 – 13	13 – 15
Beets, large	20 – 25	25 – 30
Bok Choy	5-7	7-8
Broccoli, flowerets	2 – 3	3 – 4
Broccoli, stalks	3 – 4	4 – 5
Brussel sprouts	3 – 4	4 – 5
Cabbage, red, purple or green	2 – 3	3 – 4
Carrots, slices	1 – 2	2 – 3
Carrots, whole	2 – 3	3 – 4
Cauliflower, flowerets	2 – 3	3 – 4
Cauliflower, whole	8	8-10
Celery, slices	2 – 3	3 – 4
Chard, Swiss	5	5-7
Chinese cabbage	5	5-7
Collard	4 – 5	5 – 6
Corn, kernels	1 – 2	2 – 3
Corn, on the cob	3 – 4	4 – 5
Eggplant, slices	2 – 3	3 – 4
Endive	1 – 2	2 – 3
Escarole	1 – 2	2 – 3
Leafy greens	3 – 6	4 – 7
Leeks	2 – 4	3 – 5
Mushrooms, dry	10	N/A
Mushrooms, fresh	5	5-7
Okra	2 – 3	3 – 4
Onions	2 – 3	3 – 4
Parsnips	1 – 2	2 – 3
Peas	1 – 2	2 – 3
Potatoes, cubes	7 – 9	9 – 11
Potatoes, whole	12 – 15	15 – 19
Potatoes, baby	10 – 12	12 – 14

Pumpkin, small slices	4 – 5	6 – 7
Pumpkin, large slices	8 – 10	10 – 14
Rutabaga, sliced	3 – 5	4 – 6
Spinach	1 – 2	3 – 4
Squash, acorn	6 – 7	8 – 9
Squash, butternut	8 – 10	10 – 12
Sweet potato, cubes	7 – 9	9 – 11
Sweet potato, small	10 – 12	12 – 14
Sweet potato, large	12 – 15	15 – 19
Sweet pepper, slices	1 – 3	2 – 4
Tomatoes, quartered	2 – 3	4 – 5
Tomatoes, whole	3 – 5	5 – 7
Turnip	2 – 4	4 – 6
Yam, cubes	7 – 9	9 – 11
Yam, small	10 – 12	12 – 14
Yam, large	12 – 15	15 – 19
Zucchini	2 – 3	3 – 4

FRUITS	Fresh, Cooking Time in Minutes	Dried, Cooking Time in Minutes
Apples, slices	2 – 3	3 – 4
Apples, whole	3 – 4	4 – 6
Apricots	2 – 3	3 – 4
Peaches	2 – 3	4 – 5
Pears, slices	2 – 3	4 – 5
Pears, whole	3 – 4	4 – 6
Prunes	2 – 3	4 – 5
Raisins	N/A	4 – 5

MEAT	Cooking Time in Minutes
Beef, brisket	70
Beef, dressed	20 – 25
Beef, flank steak	15
Beef, ground	6
Beef, pot roast, steak, rump, round (large)	35 – 40
Beef, pot roast, steak, rump (chunks)	25 – 30
Beef, ribs	60
Beef, shanks	25 – 30
Beef, stew (cubes)	12
Beef, stock	60
Beef, tongue	50
Beef, oxtail	40 – 50
Chicken, breasts	8 – 10
Chicken, drumsticks and thighs	10 – 15
Chicken, ground	5
Chicken, liver	3
Chicken, stock (bones, etc.)	35
Chicken, strips	1
Chicken, whole (up to 4lbs)	20 – 25
Cornish Hen, whole	10 – 15
Duck, cut up with bones	10 – 12
Duck, whole	25 – 30
Goat	20
Goose, pieces	20
Ham, slices	9 – 12
Ham picnic shoulder	25 – 30
Hare	35
Lamb, cubes	10 – 15
Lamb, ground	12
Lamb, leg/shank	35 – 45
Lamb, roast	20
Lamb, shoulder	25
Lamb, stew meat	10 – 15
Pheasant	20 – 25
Pigeon	25
Pork, belly	40
Pork, butt roast	45 – 50
Pork, ground	5
Pork, leg/shank	35
Pork, loin	12
Pork, ribs	20 – 25

Pork, roast	30
Pork sausage	8
Pork, shoulder	50
Pork, stew (cubed)	8
Pork, stock (bones, etc.)	60
Quail	9
Rabbit	18
Turkey, breast, boneless	15 – 20
Turkey, breast, whole, with bones	25 – 30
Turkey, drumsticks	15 – 20
Turkey, wings	20
Veal, chops	5 – 8
Veal, ground	6
Veal, Osso buco	20
Veal, roast	35 – 45
Veal, stock (bones, etc.)	60
Veal, tongue	40

VEGETABLES & SIDE DISHES

– VEGETABLES & SIDE DISHES –

1. Potato and Wheat Berry Breakfast

Did you know that wheat berries don't require an overnight soak? You can do that, but if you are in a hurry, boil them for 1 hour before pressure cooking.

Servings 4

Ready in about 20 minutes

NUTRITIONAL INFORMATION
(Per Serving)

371 - Calories
7.3g - Fat
70.1g - Carbs
10.9g - Protein
2.2g - Sugars

Ingredients

- 5 teaspoons sesame oil
- 3 cloves garlic, smashed
- 1 medium-sized leek, peeled and sliced
- 7 cups water
- 2 ¼ cups white wheat berries, soaked overnight
- 5 medium-sized potatoes, cubed
- 1/4 teaspoon ground black pepper, or more to taste
- 1 teaspoon seasoned salt
- 1 teaspoon dried thyme

Directions

1. Combine the white wheat berries with water in your Instant Pot.
2. In a medium-sized skillet, warm the sesame oil over medium-high flame. Then, sauté the leeks and garlic until tender. Stir in the thyme; cook for 1 more minute, stirring a few times.
3. Choose "Multi-grain" function; cook your wheat together with potatoes for about 20 minutes.
4. When the mixture is ready, add sautéed leeks with garlic.
5. Sprinkle with seasoned salt and black pepper to taste. Serve.

– VEGETABLES & SIDE DISHES –

2. Egg and Spinach Cup Custards

Fresh or dried dill weed is the key player in seasoning these fluffy custard cups for the perfect beginning of your day. You can serve them with sour cream and a homemade crusty bread.

Servings 4

Ready in about 8 minutes

NUTRITIONAL INFORMATION
(Per Serving)

177 - Calories
9.8g - Fat
9.1g - Carbs
13.9g - Protein
7.5g - Sugars

Ingredients

- 2 ½ cups milk
- 6 large-sized eggs
- 1 teaspoon dill weed
- 1/3 teaspoon salt
- 1 teaspoon cayenne pepper
- 1/3 teaspoon ground black pepper, or more to your liking
- 2 ½ cups baby spinach, chopped

Directions

1. Set the pressure cooker rack in the cooker; pour in 3 cups water.
2. Beat the eggs in a mixing bowl until frothy; now add the rest of the ingredients.
3. Divide the mixture among four heat-safe ramekins. Cover the ramekins with foil tightly. Lock the lid onto the pot. Set the machine to cook at HIGH pressure. Cook for about 8 minutes.
4. Use the quick-release method and open the cooker. Transfer the ramekins to a wire rack to cool before serving. Serve at once.

3. Cauliflower and Anchovy Salad

Serve this crisp and flavorful salad with a main course or enjoy it as an appetizer or a light healthy dinner. This is the best chilled overnight. Doubtless, it's easy to add plenty of veggies to every meal!

Servings 6

Ready in about 5 minutes

NUTRITIONAL INFORMATION
(Per Serving)

104 - Calories
8.0g - Fat
5.4g - Carbs
3.8g - Protein
3.7g - Sugars

Ingredients

For the Salad:
- 3/4 cup water
- 2 cups cauliflower florets
- 1 large-sized orange, peeled and sliced thinly

For the Vinaigrette:
- 3 tablespoons extra-virgin olive oil
- 3 anchovies
- 1/3 tablespoon capers
- 1 teaspoon salt
- 1/2 hot pepper, finely chopped
- 1/2 teaspoon black pepper, or more to taste
- 1/2 lemon, zested and squeezed

Directions

1. Add cauliflower and water to the cooker. Close and lock the lid. Press "Manual" and choose 5-minute pressure cooking time.
2. Meanwhile, make your vinaigrette by combining all the ingredients together.
3. When time is up, open the cooker according to manufacturer's instructions.
4. Dress the cauliflower with the vinaigrette; garnish with orange slices and serve chilled.

– VEGETABLES & SIDE DISHES –

4. Broccoli and Pineapple Salad

Broccoli is a powerhouse of many valuable nutrients. This amazing vegetable fights cancer and boosts the immune system. It reduces allergic reaction and protects your cardiovascular system. Enjoy!

Servings 6

Ready in about 6 minutes

NUTRITIONAL INFORMATION
(Per Serving)

121 - Calories
7.4g - Fat
13.1g - Carbs
3.6g - Protein
5.9g - Sugars

Ingredients

For the Salad:
- 3/4 cup water
- 2 ½ cups broccoli florets
- 1 large-sized carrot, thinly sliced
- 1/2 cup pineapple, peeled and sliced thinly

For the Vinaigrette:
- 3 tablespoons extra-virgin olive oil
- 3/4 orange, zested and squeezed
- 1 teaspoon fresh basil, roughly chopped
- 1/2 teaspoon white pepper, or more to taste
- 1 teaspoon kosher salt
- 1/4 teaspoon cayenne pepper
- 1 ½ tablespoons fresh cilantro, roughly chopped

Directions

1. In your Instant Pot, place carrots, broccoli, and water. Then, lock the cooker's lid. Choose "Manual" and 6-minute pressure cooking time.
2. To make the vinaigrette, thoroughly mix all the vinaigrette components.
3. Afterwards, open your cooker according to manufacturer's instructions.
4. Dress the salad and garnish with pineapple slices; serve chilled.

– VEGETABLES & SIDE DISHES –

5. Greek-Style Wheat Berries

Wheat berries are packed with fiber, protein, and minerals such as magnesium, copper, selenium, etc. To make your meal more unique, serve with high-quality Greek yogurt and pitted Kalamata olives.

Servings 4

Ready in about 25 minutes

NUTRITIONAL INFORMATION
(Per Serving)

127 - Calories
4.0g - Fat
21.2g - Carbs
3.5g - Protein
1.8g - Sugars

Ingredients

- 1 tablespoon olive oil
- 1 large-sized carrot, thinly sliced
- 3/4 cup red onions, peeled and sliced
- 1/2 cup celery, chopped
- 1 ½ cups wheat berries, soaked overnight
- 1/4 teaspoon ground black pepper
- 1 teaspoon sea salt

Directions

1. In the Instant Pot, combine white wheat berries with 7 cups water.
2. Place a sauté pan over medium heat; warm the oil and sauté red onions until tender and translucent. Add salt and ground black pepper to your liking.
3. Next, add the carrots and celery. Press the "Multigrain" button; cook everything until tender or about 25 minutes. Now, add sautéed onions.
4. Serve topped with Greek yogurt and Greek olives. Enjoy!

– VEGETABLES & SIDE DISHES –

6. Summer Quinoa Salad

Quinoa, cherry tomatoes, and cucumber are tossed with a high-quality white cheese for a quick and protein-packed dinner or appetizer.

Servings 4

Ready in about
8 minutes
+ chilling time

NUTRITIONAL
INFORMATION
(Per Serving)

285 - Calories
6.7g - Fat
35.2g - Carbs
11.6g - Protein
2.5g - Sugars

Ingredients

- 1 ¾ cups water
- 1 ½ cups white quinoa, well-rinsed
- 1 ¼ cups cherry tomatoes, quartered
- 1/2 teaspoon kosher salt
- 1 large-sized cucumber, thinly sliced
- 3/4 cup green onions, sliced
- 2 teaspoons apple cider vinegar
- 2 teaspoons lemon zest
- 1/3 cup Feta cheese, crumbled

Directions

1. In the Instant Pot, place the quinoa, lemon zest, salt, and water.
2. Then, lock the lid of your cooker. Choose the "Manual" and 8-minute pressure cooking time.
3. Rinse and fluff the quinoa and transfer to a bowl. Let it cool completely.
4. Add the rest of the ingredients to the chilled quinoa. Gently stir to combine and serve.

– VEGETABLES & SIDE DISHES –

7. Cannellini Salad with Peppers and Carrots

Did you know that cannellini beans can help you lose weight? Therefore, this healthy and nutritious salad is easy to fit into your diet plan. To serve, you can spoon the salad into crisp lettuce leaves.

Servings 4

Ready in about 20 minutes

NUTRITIONAL INFORMATION
(Per Serving)

257 - Calories
4.2g - Fat
42.8g - Carbs
14.8g - Protein
5.4g - Sugars

Ingredients

- 4 ¼ cups water
- 1 ¼ cups dry cannellini beans, soaked
- 3 garlic cloves, smashed
- 3/4 cup green onions, chopped
- 1/2 cup carrots, thinly sliced
- 2 bell peppers, deveined and thinly sliced
- 1 ½ tablespoons sherry vinegar
- 3 teaspoons olive oil
- 1/2 teaspoon sea salt
- 1/4 teaspoon ground black pepper
- 1 ½ teaspoons sage
- 2 sprigs thyme
- 1/4 cup fresh cilantro

Directions

1. Add the soaked beans, water, green onions, and smashed garlic to the cooker.
2. Close and lock the lid. Press the "Manual" button and choose 20-minute pressure cooking time.
3. Then, open the cooker using natural pressure release. Strain the beans and add the rest of the ingredients. Serve and enjoy!

– VEGETABLES & SIDE DISHES –

8. Tender Vegetables with Walnuts

This vegetable dish is definitely one of the best options to make you luncheon a delicious pleasure. In this recipe, you can substitute almonds for walnuts with the same result.

Servings 4

Ready in about 10 minutes

NUTRITIONAL INFORMATION (Per Serving)

228 - Calories
18.9g - Fat
14.4g - Carbs
3.8g - Protein
4.8g - Sugars

Ingredients

- 2 cups eggplant, peeled and cubed
- 1 ½ teaspoons sea salt
- 4 tablespoons olive oil
- 1 cup potatoes, peeled and cubed
- 1/2 cup red onions, thinly sliced
- 1/2 cup carrots, thinly sliced
- 1/4 cup fresh basil, chopped
- 1 ½ cups tomatoes, diced
- 1/4 cup walnuts, toasted and coarsely chopped

Directions

1. Coat the eggplant cubes with sea salt; then, place the eggplant in a strainer and let stand for 27-28 minutes.
2. Choose the "Sauté" function; warm the olive oil and cook the eggplant, carrots, red onion, and the potatoes until they have softened.
3. Stir in the tomatoes and basil leaves. Now choose the "Manual" function; use 10-minute cooking time.
4. Serve immediately sprinkled with toasted walnuts.

– VEGETABLES & SIDE DISHES –

9. Creamy Vegetable Soup

This colorful and hearty soup will nourish and energize your body and soul. Serve with freshly grated Colby cheese, if desired.

Servings 6

Ready in about 35 minutes

NUTRITIONAL INFORMATION
(Per Serving)

206 - Calories
0.9g - Fat
43.8g - Carbs
6.7g - Protein
4.7g - Sugars

Ingredients

- 1/2 cup yellow onions, chopped
- 1/2 cup spinach leaves, chopped
- 1/2 cup parsnip, finely chopped
- 1/2 cup carrots, sliced
- 7 potatoes, peeled and diced
- 1/2 cup celery stalk, thinly sliced
- 1/2 teaspoon ground black pepper, to taste
- 1/2 teaspoon salt
- 1/2 teaspoon paprika
- 2 ½ cups chicken broth
- Colby cheese, for garnish

Directions

1. Simply place all of the above ingredients, except the Colby cheese, into your Instant Pot. Now press the "Soup" key; adjust the timer to 35 minutes.
2. Blend the soup with an immersion blender. Serve the soup in individual bowls topped with the grated cheese. Enjoy

– VEGETABLES & SIDE DISHES –

10. Pureed Cauliflower Soup with Cheese

Looking for hearty, creamed soup? This silky and cheesy soup is sure to please everyone! Adding freshly grated Cheddar cheese gives this soup a creamy texture and wonderful taste. Enjoy!

Servings 6

Ready in about 35 minutes

NUTRITIONAL INFORMATION
(Per Serving)

125 - Calories
6.8g - Fat
8.9g - Carbs
7.7g - Protein
3.8g - Sugars

Ingredients

- 1 celery stalks, thinly sliced
- 3 carrots, sliced
- 1/2 cup parsnip, finely chopped
- 2 ½ cups cauliflower florets
- 1/2 teaspoon ground black pepper
- 1/2 teaspoon salt
- 1/3 teaspoon paprika
- 2 cups vegetable broth
- 1 cup freshly grated Cheddar cheese, for garnish

Directions

1. Place all of the above ingredients, except the Cheddar cheese, in your Instant Pot.
2. Next, press the "Soup" key; adjust the timer to 35 minutes.
3. Blend the soup with an immersion blender. Serve the soup in individual bowls topped with grated Cheddar cheese. Enjoy!

– VEGETABLES & SIDE DISHES –

11. Vegetarian Mushroom Stew

Here's one of the best winter-worthy stews that is chock full of protein packed mushrooms, amazing root veggies and aromatic seasonings. Sure, you don't have to wait for winter to try this recipe!

Servings 8

Ready in about 40 minutes

NUTRITIONAL INFORMATION (Per Serving)

168 - Calories
3.6g - Fat
28.8g - Carbs
7.5g - Protein
5.8g - Sugars

Ingredients

- 1 ½ tablespoons vegetable oil
- 1 teaspoon minced garlic
- 1/2 cup green bell peppers, seeded and coarsely chopped
- 1/2 cup red bell peppers, seeded and coarsely chopped
- 24 ounces mushrooms, thinly sliced
- 1 cup onions, chopped
- 5 potatoes, chopped
- 1 celery stalk, chopped
- 1 carrot, chopped
- 1/3 teaspoon fennel seeds
- 1/2 teaspoon paprika
- 1 teaspoon sea salt
- 1/4 teaspoon freshly cracked black pepper
- 1/2 teaspoon celery seeds
- 1 bay leaf
- 3 tablespoons tomato paste
- 3 cups vegetable broth
- 2 ½ tablespoons arrowroot flour

Directions

1. Press the "Sauté" button on your Instant Pot. Now, sauté the onion, garlic, and mushrooms until they are tender.
2. Stir in the rest of the ingredients, minus the arrowroot flour. Cover and press the "Meat/ Stew" button.
3. Cook for 40 minutes using HIGH pressure.
4. Then, make the slurry. Whisk the arrowroot flour with 1/3 of the cooking liquid. Add the slurry back to the cooker. Serve hot and enjoy.

– VEGETABLES & SIDE DISHES –

12. Summer Tomato-Potato Soup

Summer is the perfect time to enjoy tomatoes! Tomatoes are a nutritional powerhouse loaded with essential vitamins, minerals, antioxidants, and fiber.

Servings 6

Ready in about 28 minutes

NUTRITIONAL INFORMATION
(Per Serving)

191 - Calories
5.8g - Fat
32.8g - Carbs
4.7g - Protein
9.5g - Sugars

Ingredients

- 2 ½ tablespoons butter
- 3 yellow potatoes, diced
- 1 cup parsnip, chopped
- 2 small-sized carrots, thinly sliced
- 1 cup onions, chopped
- 2 ½ pounds fresh tomatoes, chopped
- 1 teaspoon cayenne pepper
- 1/3 teaspoon salt
- 1/2 teaspoon ground black pepper
- 3 teaspoons fresh marjoram leaves, finely minced
- 3 ½ cups vegetable stock

Directions

1. Melt the butter in a cooker turned to the Sauté function. Add the onion, carrot, parsnip, and potato; cook, stirring often, until the onion turns translucent, about 6 minutes.
2. Stir in the tomatoes, broth, dill, oregano, salt, and pepper.
3. Lock the cooker's lid onto the pot. Set the machine to cook at HIGH pressure. Set the machine's timer for 27-28 minutes.
4. Turn off the Instant Pot. Allow the pressure to return to normal gradually. Unlock and open the cooker.
5. Then, puree the mixture into a thick soup using an immersion blender. Serve hot.

– VEGETABLES & SIDE DISHES –

13. Red Cabbage with Apples

Enjoy this perfectly cooked red cabbage with sweet apples and cooking wine. Sangiovese-based wine goes well for this recipe. Serve alongside a corn on the cob or fresh salad.

Servings 4

Ready in about 30 minutes

NUTRITIONAL INFORMATION
(Per Serving)

202 - Calories
5.6g - Fat
29.1g - Carbs
2.3g - Protein
16.9g - Sugars

Ingredients

- 1 ½ tablespoons bacon fat
- 1 ½ cups tart apples, peeled, cored and diced
- 2 cups red cabbage, shredded and stems removed
- 1/2 cup onions, diced
- 1 ¼ cups beef stock
- 3/4 cup dry red wine
- 1/3 cup apple cider vinegar
- 2 ½ tablespoons all-purpose flour
- 2 tablespoons brown sugar, light or dark
- 1/2 teaspoon sea salt
- 1/4 teaspoon ground black pepper
- 1/4 teaspoon ground cloves
- 1 teaspoon dried thyme
- 1 ½ tablespoons cornstarch dissolved in 4 tablespoons dry red wine

Directions

1. Set your Instant Pot to "Sauté". Warm bacon fat until it is completely melted. Then, sauté the onion and apples until soft, approximately 8 minutes. Hit the "Cancel" button.
2. Add the cabbage, apple cider vinegar, red wine, stock, ground black pepper, thyme, sea salt, ground cloves, and brown sugar.
3. Dust with flour; gently stir to combine. Select "Manual" and cook 8 minutes. Perform a quick-release for 5 minutes.
4. Next, push the "Sauté" and bring the mixture to a boil; add the prepared cornstarch slurry. Allow it to boil for about 7 minutes, or until cooking liquids are thickened. Serve warm.

– VEGETABLES & SIDE DISHES –

14. Mediterranean Tomato Risotto

High-quality rice, vegetables and carefully selected spices are magically transformed into a hearty Mediterranean-style risotto that is healthy as well. This recipe is both easy and sophisticated. Enjoy!

Servings 6

Ready in about 25 minutes

NUTRITIONAL INFORMATION
(Per Serving)

354 - Calories
8.0g - Fat
49.3g - Carbs
6.5g - Protein
2.3g - Sugars

Ingredients

- 2 ½ tablespoons olive oil, softened
- 2 carrots, grated
- 1 cup tomato purée
- 2 ½ cups brown rice
- 2 bay leaves
- 1/4 teaspoon freshly cracked black pepper
- 1 teaspoon salt
- 1/2 teaspoon red pepper, crushed

Directions

1. First, add 2 cups of water to your Instant Pot's inner pot.
2. Now stir in the remaining ingredients. Press the "Rice" button and cook for 25 minutes.
3. Serve and enjoy!

– VEGETABLES & SIDE DISHES –

15. Porcini Mushroom Curry

Vegetarian diet and pressure cooking go hand in hand. This great combo of lentils and vegetables proves that. Just follow these simple steps, sit down and enjoy a bowl of the best curry ever.

Servings 6

Ready in about 13 minutes

NUTRITIONAL INFORMATION
(Per Serving)

351 - Calories
6.6g - Fat
52.1g - Carbs
21.8g - Protein
7.7g - Sugars

Ingredients

- 3 cloves garlic, peeled and minced
- 1 cup bell peppers, thinly sliced
- 1 cup leeks, diced
- 2 cups porcini mushrooms, thinly sliced
- 2 ½ tablespoons curry paste
- 2 cups lentils
- 2 ½ cups vegetable stock
- 2 ½ cups soy milk
- 1 teaspoon salt
- 1/3 teaspoon celery seeds
- 1 teaspoon dried dill weed
- 1/3 teaspoon cumin seeds
- 1/2 teaspoon ground black pepper

Directions

1. Choose the "Sauté" function on your cooker. Sauté the leeks and garlic for 5 minutes or until tender.
2. Next, push the "Cancel" button. Add the curry paste, bell pepper, and porcini mushrooms; stir until everything is well combined.
3. Pour in the soy milk and stock. Stir in the remaining ingredients.
4. Close the lid and choose "Manual" setting; set the time for 8 minutes. Serve warm and enjoy!

POULTRY

– POULTRY –

16. Seasoned Chicken with Cheese

A whole chicken is always a good idea for a family lunch. Instant Pot chicken is one of the best ways to comfort yourself and your family. Enjoy!

Servings 6

Ready in about 25 minutes

NUTRITIONAL INFORMATION (Per Serving)

380 - Calories
25.1g - Fat
13.8g - Carbs
26.1g - Protein
7.0g - Sugars

Ingredients
- 1/4 teaspoon ground black pepper, or more to taste
- 3/4 teaspoon kosher salt
- 2 ½ cups whole skinless and boneless chicken, cut into bite-sized chunks
- 3 tablespoons oil
- 3 cloves garlic, minced
- 1 cup onions, finely chopped
- 1 ½ teaspoons bouillon granules
- 1 tablespoon molasses
- 1 ½ teaspoons dried basil
- 1 ½ teaspoons dried oregano
- 2 (10-ounce) cans tomato sauce
- 2 tablespoons butter, at room temperature
- 1 ½ tablespoons flour
- 1 ½ cups Cheddar cheese, grated
- 1 ¼ cups olives, pitted and halved

Directions
1. Generously season your chicken with salt and black pepper. Heat oil and sauté chicken chunks until they start to brown.
2. Add onion and garlic and sauté for 5 minutes or until they are tender. Now add tomato sauce, molasses, oregano, basil, and bouillon granules and cook an additional 5 minutes. Stir to combine.
3. Secure the lid and select the "Manual" mode. Cook for 15 minutes. Carefully remove the lid (according to the manufacturer's instructions) and add the cheese; stir to blend.
4. Combine flour and butter in a mixing bowl. Add this mixture to the Instant Pot to thicken the sauce. Serve warm garnished with olives.

– POULTRY –

17. Easiest Chicken Risotto

A perfect mix of flavor and textures in this classic chicken risotto will amaze your family and friends. Don't be shy about seasonings and enjoy experimenting with them.

Servings 4

Ready in about 18 minutes

NUTRITIONAL INFORMATION
(Per Serving)

558 - Calories
20.2g - Fat
45.1g - Carbs
41.3g - Protein
2.4g - Sugars

Ingredients

- 1/3 cup butter, at room temperature
- 2 garlic cloves, chopped
- 1 ¼ pounds chicken, diced
- 1 cup onion, chopped
- 4 ½ cups chicken stock
- 1/2 cup white wine
- 1 ½ cups rice
- 1 teaspoon sea salt
- 1 sprig rosemary
- 1/4 teaspoon freshly ground black pepper
- 1/4 cup chopped fresh parsley, for garnish

Directions

1. Use the "Sauté" function to preheat your cooker. Now warm the butter, and cook the onion, garlic, and chicken for about 5 minutes.
2. Stir in the rice and wine. Add the chicken stock, rosemary, salt, and black pepper. Use "Manual" mode, and adjust the time to 13 minutes. Give it another good stir. Now seal the lid.
3. Serve topped with fresh parsley. Enjoy!

– POULTRY –

18. Chicken and Barley Soup with Garbanzo Beans

A soul-satisfying soup just like grandma used to make. Pearl barley is very nutritious food with many health benefits. Don't forget to rinse your barley under running water before pressure cooking to wash away any debris.

Servings 8

Ready in about 17 minutes

NUTRITIONAL INFORMATION
(Per Serving)

492 - Calories
10.4g - Fat
82.3g - Carbs
21.8g - Protein
8.5g - Sugars

Ingredients

- 1 ½ tablespoons olive oil
- 1 cup onions, diced
- 4 cloves garlic, minced
- 6 Italian turkey sausage links, casings removed
- 2 bone-in chicken breast halves, skinless
- 3 ½ cups chicken stock
- 1 ½ cups water
- 2 cups pearl barley
- 18 ounces canned garbanzo beans, drained
- 20 ounces fresh spinach leaves, chopped

Directions

1. Heat 1 teaspoon olive oil in the cooker over medium heat. Add the sausage and cook until browned; crumble it and reserve.
2. Add another teaspoon of olive oil to the pressure cooker; cook minced garlic and onion for 5 minutes; add the barley and stir 2 minutes more.
3. Return the sausage to the Instant Pot. Add the chicken, water, and chicken stock to the cooker, too. Close the lid securely and cook over high heat for 10 minutes.
4. Remove the cooker from heat; use a quick-release method. Add the spinach and garbanzo beans, and heat through before serving.

– POULTRY –

19. Mom's Chicken Soup

This hearty, old-fashioned chicken soup is both dinner-worthy and healthy lunch option. In addition, the soup is loaded with fresh vegetables that are chock-full of valuable nutrients.

Servings 6

Ready in about 33 minutes

NUTRITIONAL INFORMATION
(Per Serving)

287 - Calories
6.7g - Fat
27.1g - Carbs
28.2g - Protein
4.0g - Sugars

Ingredients

- 3 celery stalks, chopped
- 1 cup white onions, peeled and diced
- 4 potatoes, diced
- 1 pound chicken breasts, boneless, skinless and chopped
- 2 carrots, trimmed and chopped
- 1/4 teaspoon freshly cracked black pepper, to taste
- 1/2 teaspoon salt
- 4 ¼ cups chicken broth
- 2 tablespoons fresh parsley leaves, chopped

Directions

1. Simply throw all of the above ingredients into your Instant Pot.
2. Turn "Manual" function on the cooker; set the timer for 33 minutes. Serve hot.

– POULTRY –

20. Chicken and Yogurt Curry

This chicken curry is not only easy to cook but it has a rich taste thanks to the carefully selected seasonings. Don't forget to add a pinch of ground allspice for some extra oomph!

Servings 4

Ready in about 22 minutes

NUTRITIONAL INFORMATION
(Per Serving)

266 - Calories
5.1g - Fat
30.9g - Carbs
21.9g - Protein
8.1g - Sugars

Ingredients

- 1 ½ cups chicken stock
- 4 cloves garlic, peeled and minced
- 1 ¼ cups scallions, thinly sliced
- 1/2 cup parsnip, chopped
- 2 potatoes, peeled and diced
- 1/2 cup carrot, chopped
- 1 ½ cups chicken, cut into pieces
- 1/2 teaspoon ground allspice
- 2 tablespoons red curry paste
- 1/2 teaspoon black pepper, to your liking
- 1/3 teaspoon cumin powder
- 1 teaspoon salt
- 1 cup yogurt
- 1 ½ tablespoons balsamic vinegar

Directions

1. Place all the ingredients, except the yogurt, in your cooker.
2. Cover with the lid and choose the "Meat" key; cook for 22 minutes.
3. Next, pour in the yogurt. Stir until everything is well incorporated. Serve at once.

– POULTRY –

21. Summer Chicken Chili

As one of the most important food sources on the Earth, beans are a storehouse of essential nutrients. Chicken chili is just one of many amazing recipes that include this comfort food.

Servings 8

Ready in about 20 minutes

NUTRITIONAL INFORMATION
(Per Serving)

498 - Calories
15.2g - Fat
51.9g - Carbs
35.4g - Protein
3.1g - Sugars

Ingredients

- 3 tablespoons olive oil
- 1 cup onions, chopped
- 2 pounds ground chicken
- 1/2 cup red bell peppers, chopped
- 4 cloves garlic, minced
- 30 ounces canned diced tomatoes with green chilies
- 25 ounces canned kidney beans, drained and rinsed well
- 2 ½ cups chicken broth
- 2 cups water
- 1/4 cup fresh chopped chives, for garnish

Directions

1. Choose "Sauté" function and warm the olive oil; then cook the onion, garlic, and bell pepper for about 7 minutes or until they are tender and fragrant. Stir in the ground chicken and cook until it has browned, about 5 minutes.
2. Add the remaining ingredients, except for chives. Put the lid on, and cook under HIGH pressure for 8 minutes.
3. Ladle into soup bowls and garnish with fresh chives. Enjoy!

– POULTRY –

22. Tender Garlicky Chicken

Looking for a last-minute recipe for your dinner party? These stunning chicken breasts will fit the bill! The recipe calls for white wine; you can use a crisp white wine, such as Sauvignon Blanc or Unoaked Chardonnay.

Servings 8

Ready in about 25 minutes

NUTRITIONAL INFORMATION
(Per Serving)

313 - Calories
13.1g - Fat
3.0g - Carbs
41.7g - Protein
0.8g - Sugars

Ingredients

- 1 ½ tablespoons peanut oil
- 1/3 cup chicken broth
- 2 ½ pounds chicken breasts
- 8 medium-sized garlic cloves, peeled and minced
- 1 cup red onion, diced
- 1 ½ teaspoons dried parsley
- 1/2 teaspoon paprika
- 1 teaspoon sea salt
- 2 tablespoons arrowroot flour
- 1/3 cup white wine

Directions

1. Choose the "Sauté" feature. Cook the onions for about 7 to 8 minutes.
2. Stir in the remaining ingredients, except for the arrowroot flour; secure the lid on the Instant Pot. Select the "Poultry" button and cook for 10 minutes.
3. Make the slurry by mixing 1/3 cup of juice from the pot with the arrowroot flour. Add the slurry to the pot and cook an additional 5 minutes. Enjoy!

– POULTRY –

23. Hot Dinner Stew

Your guest will ever guess that this stew hasn't simmered all day. This amazing chicken stew is ready in 25 minutes or less, so you can get dinner on the table quickly and effortlessly.

Servings 6

Ready in about 25 minutes

NUTRITIONAL INFORMATION (Per Serving)

392 - Calories
12.2g - Fat
44.2g - Carbs
27.1g - Protein
5.7g - Sugars

Ingredients

- 2 ½ tablespoons sesame oil
- 2 cloves garlic, finely minced
- 7 boneless, skinless chicken thighs, trimmed and halved
- 1 can canned mild green chilies, chopped
- 2 small-sized onions, chopped
- 1/2 teaspoon dried basil
- 7 potatoes, quartered
- 1/3 tablespoon ground cumin
- 1/2 teaspoon dried oregano
- 2 ½ cups chicken stock

Directions

1. Heat the sesame oil in in your Instant Pot turned on the "Sauté" function. Add the chicken thighs and cook until they're lightly browned, about 5 minutes, turning once or twice. Reserve.
2. Sauté the onion until softened, about 4 minutes. Stir in the remaining ingredients. Return the reserved chicken thighs to the pot. Lock the lid onto the pot.
3. Set the machine to cook at HIGH pressure for 16 minutes. Use the quick-release function. Serve hot.

– POULTRY –

24. Red Curry Chicken Thighs

Instant Pot electric pressure cooker turns chicken thighs into an exotic, creamy meal that everyone will love! Red curry, also known as "spicy curry", is an ingredient that is commonly used in Thai cooking.

Servings 6

Ready in about 25 minutes

NUTRITIONAL INFORMATION
(Per Serving)

421 - Calories
20.2g - Fat
5.9g - Carbs
50.5g - Protein
3.1g - Sugars

Ingredients

- 2 ½ tablespoons canola oil
- 1 cup red onions, chopped
- 2 ¼ pounds boneless, skinless chicken thighs, trimmed
- 2 tablespoons red curry paste
- 1 tablespoon light brown sugar
- 2 tablespoons tomato paste
- 3/4 tablespoon fresh ginger, minced
- 1 cup chicken broth

Directions

1. Use a fork to whisk the curry paste, tomato paste, ginger, and canola oil until you have a thick paste; set aside.
2. Heat the oil using the Sauté function. Now sauté the onions and cook, stirring frequently, until softened, about 7 minutes.
3. Add the chicken thighs and stir until coated with the paste. Add the chicken broth and brown sugar. Lock the lid onto the pot. Set the machine to cook at HIGH pressure. Set the machine's timer to cook for 13 minutes.
4. Use the quick-release method. Cook, stirring frequently, for 3 to 5 minutes. To serve, pour the sauce over the chicken.

– POULTRY –

25. Pasta with Chicken and Raisins

Here's a great, luscious combo of unsmoked Italian bacon, boneless chicken and sweet raisins. It's no shocker that pasta is one of the most popular dishes in the world!

Servings 6

Ready in about 16 minutes

NUTRITIONAL INFORMATION (Per Serving)

576 - Calories
30.2g - Fat
10.8g - Carbs
62.5g - Protein
6.4g - Sugars

Ingredients

- 1 teaspoon olive oil
- 2 celery stalks, trimmed and chopped
- 2 ¼ pounds boneless, skinless chicken thighs, chopped
- 2 carrots, trimmed and diced
- 1 cup onions, diced
- 2 ½ tablespoons butter
- 2 cups chicken stock
- 1/3 cup Chardonnay
- 10 ounces pancetta chunk, chopped
- 1/4 teaspoon grated nutmeg
- 1/4 teaspoon ground black pepper
- 1/3 teaspoon salt
- 1 ½ pounds dried pasta of choice, cooked and drained
- 2 tablespoons tomato paste
- 1/4 cup raisins

Directions

1. Warm the butter and the oil in your Instant Pot using the Sauté function. Add the pancetta, onion, carrot, and celery stalk; cook, stirring frequently, until the onion becomes translucent, about 6-7 minutes.
2. Cook the chicken thighs, stirring periodically, until they have lost their raw color, about 5 minutes. Pour in the wine, scraping up any browned bits.
3. Add the stock, raisins, tomato paste, salt, black pepper, and nutmeg; stir until everything is well incorporated. Lock the lid onto the pot.
4. Set the machine to cook at HIGH pressure. Cook for 6 minutes. Lastly, use the quick-release method to bring the pressure back to normal. Serve warm over the cooked pasta.

– POULTRY –

26. Festive Chicken with Beans

Here's a heavenly delicious combination of poultry and beans! Serrano peppers are perfect for this meal and you can find them in yellow, orange, red, and brown color.

Servings 6

Ready in about 25 minutes

NUTRITIONAL INFORMATION
(Per Serving)

315 - Calories
15.4g - Fat
12.2g - Carbs
38.7g - Protein
3.6g - Sugars

Ingredients

- 2 ½ tablespoons canola oil
- 1/2 serrano pepper, seeded and diced
- 1 ½ pounds dried beans
- 1 cup tomatoes, diced
- 3/4 cup red onion, diced
- 1 ½ pounds whole chicken, cut into pieces
- 1/4 cup white wine
- 1 quart chicken broth
- 1 teaspoon smoked paprika
- 1/2 teaspoon freshly ground pepper, or more to your liking
- 1 teaspoon sea salt
- 3 cloves garlic, peeled and minced
- 1/4 cup fresh cilantro, chopped

Directions

1. Press the "Sauté" button and heat the oil. Then, sear the chicken on all sides, stirring periodically. In the pan drippings, sauté the onions, garlic, and serrano pepper.
2. Add the remaining ingredients; add the chicken back to the cooker. Place the lid on the cooker. Press the "Bean" button and cook for 25 minutes.
3. Next, remove the lid according to manufacturer's directions. Serve warm and enjoy!

– POULTRY –

27. Chicken in Herbed Lemon Sauce

Who says chicken can't be classy? This is nice spooned over polenta or a tube pasta such as penne.

Servings 6

Ready in about 27 minutes + marinating time

NUTRITIONAL INFORMATION (Per Serving)

268 - Calories
12.4g - Fat
2.6g - Carbs
33.4g - Protein
1.0g - Sugars

Ingredients

- 1 ½ pounds chicken, cut into pieces
- 1 ¼ cups water
- 1/4 cup white wine
- 1 ½ tablespoons fresh rosemary, chopped
- 1 tablespoon fresh thyme, chopped
- 1/4 cup extra-virgin olive oil
- 1 teaspoon sea salt
- 1 tablespoon fresh sage, chopped
- 1/2 teaspoon ground black pepper, to your liking
- 2 garlic cloves, minced
- Juice of 2 lemons

Directions

1. To make the marinade: in a mixing bowl, place the lemon juice, garlic, sage, thyme, rosemary, olive oil, salt, and black pepper. Mix to combine well.
2. Place the chicken pieces in the marinade. Then, leave to marinate, covered, at least 2 to 3 hours in the refrigerator
3. Press the "Sauté" key to preheat the cooker. Cook the chicken pieces for about 7 minutes, turning periodically.
4. Deglaze your pot with white wine and cook until it has evaporated. Add the chicken back to the pot along with marinade. Pour in water.
5. Press the "Manual" and cook for 15 more minutes. Next, take the chicken out of the Instant Pot.
6. Press "Sauté" and cook for 5 minutes in order to thicken the sauce. Garnish with fresh lemon slices if desired and enjoy!

– POULTRY –

28. Family Baked Chicken

The combination of ginger root, soy sauce and wine is marvelous! However, baked chicken goes with another combo of spices and ingredients. Serve with wide egg noodles.

Servings 6

Ready in about 30 minutes

NUTRITIONAL INFORMATION
(Per Serving)

387 - Calories
14.0g - Fat
5.9g - Carbs
55.3g - Protein
3.1g - Sugars

Ingredients

- 1 (2 ½ pounds) whole chicken
- 1 (1-inch) piece of ginger, minced
- 1 ½ tablespoons sugar
- 1/4 teaspoon ground black pepper
- 1/2 cup shallot, minced
- 1 teaspoon salt
- 2 tablespoons wine
- 1 ½ tablespoons soy sauce

Directions

1. Sprinkle the chicken with sugar and 1/2 teaspoon of salt. Cover the bottom of the inner pot with the remaining 1/2 teaspoon of salt.
2. Lay the chicken in the inner pot. Now, add black pepper, ginger, soy sauce, and wine.
3. Choose the "Poultry" mode and cook for 30 minutes. Serve with minced shallot and enjoy!

– POULTRY –

29. Crispy Chicken Wings with Herbed Sauce

Here're classic sticky wings! Wings cook quicker than the other parts of the chicken, so please pay special attention to the timing to avoid overcooking.

Servings 6

Ready in about 30 minutes

NUTRITIONAL INFORMATION
(Per Serving)

255 - Calories
2.6g - Fat
35.8g - Carbs
23.2g - Protein
35.1g - Sugars

Ingredients

- 1 ¼ cups chicken broth
- 1 ¼ teaspoons garlic powder
- 1/3 teaspoon cumin powder
- 1 tablespoon marjoram
- 1 teaspoon coriander
- 2 tablespoons balsamic vinegar
- 14 chicken wings
- 1/2 teaspoon ground black pepper, to your liking
- 1 teaspoon salt
- 3/4 cup honey

Directions

1. Preheat the oven to 400 degrees F. Lay the chicken wings in the Instant Pot. Place the lid on and select the "Poultry" function; cook for 10 minutes. Reserve the liquid.
2. Transfer the chicken wings to the oven; then, roast them for 5 minutes until they are crispy. Remove the chicken from the oven and reserve.
3. To make the sauce: add all the other ingredients to the pot; select the "Sauté" button and cook for about 13 minutes, stirring often. Serve the chicken wings with the sauce on the side.

– POULTRY –

30. Creamed Chicken with Yogurt Sauce

You can use fresh, ripe tomatoes when they're in season. This refreshing and spiced soup is chock-full of flavor and valuable nutrients.

Servings 6

Ready in about 18 minutes + marinating time

NUTRITIONAL INFORMATION (Per Serving)

418 - Calories
18.8g - Fat
7.6g - Carbs
51.8g - Protein
4.4g - Sugars

Ingredients

- 2 ½ tablespoons peanut oil
- 16 ounces canned tomatoes, diced
- 1/2 teaspoon ground ginger
- 1/3 teaspoon ground turmeric
- 3/4 teaspoon paprika
- 1/3 teaspoon ground black pepper
- 1 teaspoon salt
- 1/3 cup chicken broth
- 2 ¼ pounds boneless, skinless chicken thighs, trimmed
- 1 tablespoon fresh ginger, minced
- 1/2 cup plain yogurt
- 2 cloves garlic, minced
- 1 cup onion, chopped
- 1 ½ tablespoons Garam masala
- 2 tablespoons loosely packed fresh cilantro leaves, chopped

Directions

1. Combine the yogurt, paprika, ground ginger, turmeric, salt, and black pepper in a large-sized bowl.
2. Add the chicken thighs and toss until they are well coated. Then, refrigerate for at least 1 hour, turning occasionally.
3. Heat the peanut oil in a cooker turned to the browning function. Stir in the onion; sauté, stirring often, until translucent, approximately 3 minutes.
4. Stir the garlic, fresh ginger, and Garam masala until fragrant; add the tomatoes and chicken broth. Lock the lid onto the pot.
5. Set the machine to cook at HIGH pressure for 16 minutes. Reduce the pressure. Serve warm, garnished cilantro leaves.

– POULTRY –

31. Curried Turkey Soup

With this recipe, you can have all the flavor of a long-simmering turkey soup in just 25 minutes. Okra, also known as ladies' fingers, is a powerhouse of antioxidants, pyridoxine, vitamin-K, minerals and so on.

Servings 4

Ready in about 25 minutes

NUTRITIONAL INFORMATION
(Per Serving)

188 - Calories
8.3g - Fat
15.8g - Carbs
13.3g - Protein
7.6g - Sugars

Ingredients

- 2 carrots, chopped
- 1/2 pound turkey breast, chopped
- 8 ounces sugar snap peas
- 2 ½ cups water
- 8 ounces okra, frozen
- 1/2 teaspoon ground ginger
- 1/2 cup almond milk
- 1/3 teaspoon curry powder

Directions

1. Place all the ingredients into your Instant Pot.
2. Choose "Soup" mode and cook for 25 minutes.
3. Divide among individual soup bowls and serve hot.

– POULTRY –

32. Balsamic Turkey Wings

Turkey wings are a staple in the pressure cooker kitchen and they cook easily in your Instant pot. This is a dish that usually takes hours, but in the Instant pot, it's ready in a fraction of the time.

Servings 4

Ready in about 10 minutes

NUTRITIONAL INFORMATION
(Per Serving)

329 - Calories
8.9g - Fat
7.5g - Carbs
51.0g - Protein
0.0g - Sugars

Ingredients

- 1/3 cup water
- 1 ¼ cups chicken stock
- 1/2 teaspoon ground black pepper
- 1 teaspoon dried rosemary
- 1 teaspoon sea salt
- 4 tablespoons flour
- 1 teaspoon dried sage
- 3 cloves garlic, minced
- 1/4 cup balsamic vinegar
- 1 ½ pounds turkey thighs

Directions

1. Set the cooker to "Sauté"; brown the turkey thighs. Add the chicken stock and balsamic vinegar.
2. Choose the "Poultry" setting and cook turkey for 55 minutes.
3. Reserve prepared turkey thighs.
4. To make the sauce, whisk the garlic, rosemary, sage, salt, black pepper, flour and water. Whisk the flour mixture into the cooking liquid.
5. Turn your Instant Pot to "Keep/Warm" setting and simmer the sauce for 13 minutes. Serve the thighs with the sauce on the side.

– POULTRY –

33. Turkey and Bean Chili

What could be better that rich, sinfully delicious chili that is ready in 20 minutes? Indulge yourself with this restaurant-style dish!

Servings 8

Ready in about 20 minutes

NUTRITIONAL INFORMATION
(Per Serving)

319 - Calories
17.9g - Fat
11.7g - Carbs
33.7g - Protein
1.8g - Sugars

Ingredients

- 2 pounds ground turkey
- 1 cup leeks, chopped
- 2 cups water
- 2 (15-ounce) cans diced tomatoes with green chilies
- 24 ounces canned beans, drained and rinsed well
- 2 ½ cups chicken stock
- 3 tablespoons vegetable oil
- 1 teaspoon chili powder
- Sharp Cheddar cheese, shredded

Directions

1. First, heat the oil in your cooker. Add the leek and sauté for 6 minutes. Add the ground turkey and cook until the meat has browned or about 8 minutes.
2. Add the rest of the above ingredients, except for Cheddar cheese. Cover and cook under HIGH pressure for 6 minutes.
3. Ladle into soup bowls and serve topped with shredded Cheddar cheese. Enjoy!

– POULTRY –

34. Sausage and Garbanzo Bean Stew

Here's a flavorsome combo of Italian sausage, chicken meat, and canned beans that is cooked to perfection in this revolutionary programmable cooker. With a fresh salad, it is a complete meal!

Servings 6

Ready in about 35 minutes

NUTRITIONAL INFORMATION (Per Serving)

617 - Calories
12.8g - Fat
70.52g - Carbs
27.3g - Protein
8.6g - Sugars

Ingredients

- 6 Italian turkey sausage links, casings removed
- 2 bone-in chicken breast halves, skinless
- 20 ounces canned garbanzo beans, drained
- 1/2 teaspoon ground black pepper, or more to your liking
- 4 cloves garlic, minced
- 1 teaspoon salt
- 1 tablespoon canola oil
- 1 ½ cups pearl barley
- 1 cup onions, diced
- 1 ½ cups kale leaves, chopped
- 3/4 cup mild salsa
- 3 ½ cups chicken stock

Directions

1. Press the "Sauté" button. Heat canola oil. Stir in turkey sausage and cook until browned or about 5 minutes.
2. Reserve the sausage. Now, cook the garlic and onion in pan drippings until they are tender or for 5 more minutes. Add the barley and cook 2 more minutes, stirring frequently.
3. Add reserved sausage back to your cooker. Add chicken and chicken stock to the cooker.
4. Close the lid securely; place pressure regulator on vent pipe. Choose "Soup" function and cook 23 minutes. Then, allow pressure to drop on its own.
5. Next, remove chicken from the pot; shred meat and add it back to your soup. Add garbanzo beans, kale, salsa, salt, and black pepper to your liking. Serve warm and enjoy!

– POULTRY –

35. Ground Turkey Stew with Spinach

The Instant pot produces a moist and rich version of classic ground turkey stew. Serve this stew with a chunky pasta or egg noodles to amaze your guests!

Servings 8

Ready in about 20 minutes

NUTRITIONAL INFORMATION
(Per Serving)

259 - Calories
12.6g - Fat
14.4g - Carbs
22.2g - Protein
2.8g - Sugars

Ingredients

- 7 cups chicken broth
- 1 pound ground turkey
- 1 cup tomatoes, seeded and chopped
- 1 teaspoon salt
- 1 teaspoon dried thyme
- 1/2 teaspoon black pepper, to taste
- 1 teaspoon marjoram
- 1 teaspoon cayenne pepper
- 1 teaspoon dried rosemary
- 3 tablespoons butter
- 1/2 cup celery, chopped
- 1 cup onions, diced
- 1 cup carrots, diced
- 1 ½ cups spinach, chopped
- 1/3 cup white wine
- 10 ounces noodles, cooked

Directions

1. Choose the "Sauté" function. Warm the butter and brown the meat, adding the seasonings. Cook till the meat has browned, about 5 minutes.
2. Stir in the onion, carrots, and celery; cook for about 5 minutes. Add the wine to deglaze the pot.
3. Add the remaining ingredients, except the noodles; give it a good stir and cook for 10 minutes. Serve warm with cooked noodles.

PORK

– PORK –

36. Pork Sausage Gravy

After you season ground pork, you'll gently simmer it in your Instant pot. Spoon over homemade biscuits or toast.

Servings 6

Ready in about 13 minutes

NUTRITIONAL INFORMATION (Per Serving)

279 - Calories
6.4g - Fat
9.4g - Carbs
43.5g - Protein
4.3g - Sugars

Ingredients
- 1 cup beef stock
- 1/2 teaspoon celery seeds
- 1/2 teaspoon ground black pepper
- 1/3 teaspoon grated nutmeg
- 1/3 teaspoon red pepper flakes, crushed
- 1 sprig thyme
- 1 teaspoon salt
- 2 pounds lean ground pork sausage
- 5 tablespoons all-purpose flour
- 2 cups low-fat milk

Directions
1. Crumble the ground pork into the Instant Pot turned to the Sauté function; cook, stirring occasionally, until browned, approximately 4 minutes.
2. Stir in the thyme, red pepper, black pepper, nutmeg, salt, and celery seeds; cook for one more minute, until fragrant. Pour in the beef stock.
3. Lock the lid onto the pot. Cook for 5 minutes under HIGH pressure. Afterward, use the quick-release method and open the cooker. Then, bring the gravy to a simmer, stirring continuously.
4. Whisk the milk and flour in a mixing bowl or a measuring cup until the flour dissolves; add the mixture to the simmering gravy.
5. Continue cooking for about 3 minutes. Serve at once.

— PORK —

37. Savory Ham Bread Pudding

For many home chefs, this is one of their all-time favorite meals to make! It is also super easy to prepare for weeknight dinner.

Servings 6

Ready in about 23 minutes

NUTRITIONAL INFORMATION (Per Serving)

195 - Calories
10.0g - Fat
13.3g - Carbs
12.9g - Protein
4.9g - Sugars

Ingredients

- 8 slices Italian bread, torn into pieces
- 8 slices of ham
- 1 1/3 cups milk
- 3/4 tablespoon honey
- 1 tablespoon vegetable oil
- 1/2 teaspoon ground black pepper, to taste
- 1 teaspoon salt
- 4 eggs, at room temperature

Directions

1. Coat a soufflé dish with a nonstick cooking spray; set aside. Place the pressure cooker rack in the cooker; pour in 3 cups water.
2. Set a skillet over medium heat and brown the ham for about 3 minutes; chop the ham into bits. Transfer the ham to a bowl; add the bread pieces.
3. In another bowl, whisk the eggs, milk, honey, salt, and black pepper. Pour the egg mixture over the bread mixture; toss well to coat. Spoon the mixture into the buttered baking dish.
4. Cover the baking dish with a piece of parchment paper; then, seal with a piece of an aluminum foil. Make the foil sling and lower the sealed dish onto the rack in the cooker. Set the machine to cook at HIGH pressure.
5. Cook for 20 minutes. Use the quick-release method to unlock and open the cooker. Serve at room temperature.

– PORK –

38. Barbeque Pork Roast

As one of the family favorite dishes, this recipe makes the meat very tender. The recipe is very easy to make and yields even 16 servings.

Servings 16

Ready in about
1 hour 5 minutes

NUTRITIONAL
INFORMATION
(Per Serving)

282 - Calories
6.0g - Fat
9.4g - Carbs
44.6g - Protein
6.6g - Sugars

Ingredients

- 6 pounds pork butt roast
- 14 ounces barbeque sauce
- 1 teaspoon sea salt
- 1 ½ teaspoons garlic powder
- 1 ½ teaspoons onion powder
- 1/2 teaspoon black pepper

Directions

1. Season the pork with the onion and garlic powder; sprinkle with salt and pepper; then place into the cooker. Fill the cooker with enough water to cover.
2. Close the lid and bring up to HIGH pressure. Cook for 1 hour 5 minutes.
3. Use the quick-release method to drop the pressure. Next, drain off juices, reserving about 1½ cups.
4. Shred the pork and combine with barbeque sauce, adding reserved liquid. Serve at once.

– PORK –

39. Soft Peppery Carnitas

The secret to the perfect pork bits is revealed – go nicely and slowly! Pressure cooking is one of the best ways to prepare this traditional Mexican dish.

Servings 12

Ready in about 1 hour 5 minutes

NUTRITIONAL INFORMATION (Per Serving)

225 - Calories
7.3g - Fat
2.3g - Carbs
35.8g - Protein
1.0g - Sugars

Ingredients

- 3 ½ pounds boneless pork shoulder, cubed
- 2 cups beef broth
- 2 tablespoons olive oil
- 1 cup onions, roughly chopped
- 4 cloves garlic, roughly chopped
- 3 Serrano peppers, roughly chopped
- 2 fresh poblano peppers, roughly chopped
- 1/2 teaspoon fennel seeds
- 1/2 teaspoon ground cumin

Directions

1. Warm the olive oil in the cooker over medium-high heat. Brown the pork on all sides for 10 minutes.
2. Add the rest of the above ingredients.
3. Lock the lid onto the pressure cooker. Cook under MEDIUM steady pressure for about 55 minutes.
4. Carefully remove the lid according to the manufacturer's directions. Serve warm.

– PORK –

40. Sunday Pork and Mushroom Treat

Pork and mushrooms are probably one of the most convenient and versatile foods to cook in your Instant pot. If you're a fan of pork side rib, you'll love this recipe!

Ingredients

- 6 ½ cups of water
- 10 ounces mushrooms, peeled and sliced
- 1/2 teaspoon salt
- 1/2 teaspoon paprika
- 1/4 teaspoon black pepper, ground
- 1 ½ pounds pork side rib
- 1 ½ cups zucchini, cubed

Directions

1. Simply add all ingredients to the Instant Pot.
2. Press the "Soup" key. Cook for 40 minutes and serve warm.

Servings 6

Ready in about 40 minutes

NUTRITIONAL INFORMATION
(Per Serving)

177 - Calories
4.2g - Fat
2.5g - Carbs
31.5g - Protein
1.3g - Sugars

– PORK –

41. Cabbage with Barley and Meat

Here's a simple twist on the traditional way of preparing cabbage. Quick barley adds rich texture to this hearty meal. You and your family will enjoy!

Servings 6

Ready in about 33 minutes

NUTRITIONAL INFORMATION (Per Serving)

403 - Calories
5.9g - Fat
54.6g - Carbs
35.2g - Protein
10.3g - Sugars

Ingredients

- 6 ½ cups vegetable stock
- 1 pound lean ground pork
- 2 small-sized onions, finely chopped
- 4 garlic cloves, minced
- 1 ½ cups quick barley
- 1/4 pound ground beef
- 1/3 teaspoon freshly grated nutmeg
- 1/2 teaspoon dried marjoram
- 1/2 teaspoon paprika
- 1/2 teaspoon sea salt
- 1 cup parsnips, sliced
- 2 pounds cabbage, chopped
- 1 cup carrots, peeled and sliced
- 1/4 teaspoon freshly cracked black pepper to your taste
- 1 cup tomatoes, seeded and chopped

Directions

1. Press "Sauté" button and cook the beef and pork for several minutes. Drain off the excess fat; stir in the garlic and onion; continue sautéing for about 4 minutes more or until they're softened.
2. Next, add the stock, tomatoes, and barley. Choose "Soup" function; cook under HIGH pressure for about 8 minutes.
3. Perform a quick pressure release; add the remaining ingredients. Put the cooker's lid back on and press "Soup" button; bring to HIGH pressure and cook for 20 minutes. Serve warm.

– PORK –

42. Pork Sausage with Tomato and Corn

Flavorful pork sausages are made incredibly tasty thanks to the magic of the Instant pot. Use frozen corn kernels in this recipe.

Servings 6

Ready in about 25 minutes

NUTRITIONAL INFORMATION
(Per Serving)

535 - Calories
38.3g - Fat
18.7g - Carbs
29.1g - Protein
4.2g - Sugars

Ingredients

- 1 ¼ cups vegetable stock
- 3 ½ cups water
- 2 tomatoes
- 1 ¾ pounds pork sausage, sliced
- 3 ½ cups corn kernels
- 1/2 teaspoon ground black pepper, or more to taste
- 1 teaspoon salt
- 1 bay leaf

Directions

1. Simply place all the ingredients, except the corn kernels, into the inner pot of your Instant Pot.
2. Press the "Beans" button; cook for 12-13 minutes. Add the corn kernels and let them stand covered for 10 minutes.

– PORK –

43. Juicy BBQ Pork

Sometimes a true comfort food such as BBQ pork and a slice or two of homemade crusty bread is all you really need. Whether it is a family lunch or celebratory dinner, pork roast is always a good idea!

Servings 8

Ready in about 55 minutes

NUTRITIONAL INFORMATION
(Per Serving)

312 - Calories
5.2g - Fat
26.4g - Carbs
37.2g - Protein
18.6g - Sugars

Ingredients

- 2 ½ pounds pork butt roast
- 20 ounces BBQ sauce
- 1 teaspoon sea salt
- 1 ½ teaspoons cayenne pepper
- 1/2 teaspoon freshly ground black pepper, to taste
- 1 ½ teaspoons garlic powder

Directions

1. Generously season the pork with garlic powder, cayenne pepper, salt, and black pepper; place the seasoned pork roast in your Instant Pot.
2. Fill with enough water to cover the meat.
3. Close the lid and cook on HIGH pressure for 55 minutes.
4. Reserve about 1½ cups of the pot juices. Shred the pork with two forks and mix with BBQ sauce, adding reserved juice. Serve warm over mashed potatoes.

– PORK –

44. Pork and Lotus Root Soup

If you want a festive pork soup, here's an ideal option for you! Lotus root is a popular vegetable throughout Asia; it is a good source of fiber, vitamins, and minerals.

Servings 6

Ready in about 40 minutes

NUTRITIONAL INFORMATION
(Per Serving)

163 - Calories
4.0g - Fat
0.2g - Carbs
29.7g - Protein
0.0g - Sugars

Ingredients

- 6 ½ cups of water
- 10 ounces fresh lotus root, peeled and sliced
- 1 ½ pounds pork side rib
- 2 teaspoons sea salt
- 1/4 teaspoon black pepper, ground
- 1/2 teaspoon paprika

Directions

1. Simply put all ingredients into your Instant Pot.
2. Choose the "Soup" button. Cook approximately 35 minutes. Serve warm.

— PORK —

45. Root Vegetable Soup with Pork Ribs

This is the perfect soup for those days when you're craving a homemade, rich meal. Serve with garlic croutons and enjoy!

Servings 6

Ready in about 40 minutes

NUTRITIONAL INFORMATION
(Per Serving)

183 - Calories
4.5g - Fat
3.6g - Carbs
30.6g - Protein
2.0g - Sugars

Ingredients

- 5 cups vegetable stock
- 1/2 cup turnip, peeled and sliced
- 1 cup carrots, peeled and sliced
- 1 ½ pounds pork side rib
- 1/2 teaspoon paprika
- 1/4 teaspoon black pepper, ground
- 1 teaspoon sea salt
- 1/2 cup greens, diced

Directions

1. Simply put all ingredients, except for the greens, into your Instant Pot.
2. Choose the "Soup" button. Cook for approximately 35 minutes. Add the greens and stir until they're wilted.

– PORK –

46. Coconut Pork Curry

Pork curry is very versatile meal so you can just combine the vegetables you have on hand. You could also try adding some diced jalapeno peppers to give your dish an extra kick.

Servings 4

Ready in about 20 minutes

NUTRITIONAL INFORMATION (Per Serving)

493 - Calories
20.1g - Fat
44.9g - Carbs
35.7g - Protein
10.6g - Sugars

Ingredients

- 1 pound pork, cut into pieces
- 2 bell peppers, chopped
- 1 ½ cups vegetable stock
- 3 potatoes, peeled and diced
- 1 ½ tablespoons green curry paste
- 2 lemon grass stalks
- 1/2 cup parsnip, chopped
- 1 cup onions, chopped
- 4 cloves garlic, minced
- 1 cup carrots, chopped
- ½ cup coconut milk
- 1 ½ teaspoons sweet paprika
- 1/2 teaspoon ground black pepper
- 1 teaspoon salt

Directions

1. Place all the ingredients, except coconut milk, in your Instant Pot. Stir to combine.
2. Close and lock the lid; use "Meat" option and cook approximately 22 minutes.
3. While your curry is still hot, add ½ cup of coconut milk. Stir again to combine well.
4. Garnish with the fresh coriander if desired, and serve warm. Good luck!

– PORK –

47. Slow Cooker Holiday Meatloaf

No matter the style, a great meatloaf is not just about the recipe. It's also about the reliable kitchen tools. Instant pot meatloaf is one of the best holiday recipes you've ever tried!

Servings 10

Ready in about 7 hours

NUTRITIONAL INFORMATION
(Per Serving)

323 - Calories
6.3g - Fat
34.7g - Carbs
30.7g - Protein
10.5g - Sugars

Ingredients

For the Meatloaf:
- 1 cup yellow onion, finely chopped
- 1 ½ cups rice, cooked
- 1 pound ground pork
- 2 whole eggs1 pound ground lean beef
- 1 ½ cups milk
- 1/2 teaspoon ground black pepper, to taste
- 1 teaspoon salt
- 3/4 teaspoon onion powder
- 1 ½ teaspoons red pepper, crushed
- 3/4 teaspoon garlic powder

For the Topping:
- 1 cup ketchup
- 2 tablespoons brown sugar

Directions

1. Treat the inner pot with a non-stick cooking spray. Thoroughly combine all ingredients for the meatloaf.
2. Form the mixture into a round loaf; transfer it to the pot. Then, combine the ingredients for the topping. Spoon the topping over the meatloaf.
3. Close and lock the cooker's lid. Choose the "Slow Cook" key and cook for 7 hours on LOW.

– PORK –

48. Juicy Pork Belly

A tender pork belly cooks perfectly in the Instant pot. This recipe calls for simple ingredients. However, once you've got the technique down, it's easy to experiment with various ingredients.

Servings 6

Ready in about 30 minutes

NUTRITIONAL INFORMATION
(Per Serving)

303 - Calories
6.7g - Fat
5.5g - Carbs
50.2g - Protein
0.0g - Sugars

Ingredients

- 1/3 cup dry white wine
- 2 ½ cups water
- 3 whole cloves
- 1 cup shallots, peeled and chopped
- 3 cloves garlic, crushed
- 1/4 teaspoon brown sugar
- 2 ½ pounds pork belly, sliced

Directions

1. Choose the "Sauté" button on your Instant Pot. Sear the pork belly on both sides. Add the rest of the above ingredients.
2. Next, choose the "Meat" button and cook until the meat is almost falling apart, for 25 minutes. Serve warm.

– PORK –

49. BBQ Pork Ribs with Garden Vegetables

Ribs are easy and versatile Sunday dinner. Toss in whatever spices and herbs you have on hand and you cannot go wrong.

Servings 4

Ready in about 30 minutes

NUTRITIONAL INFORMATION (Per Serving)

527 - Calories
20.6g - Fat
52.2g - Carbs
31.1g - Protein
7.3g - Sugars

Ingredients

- 1 ¼ cups water
- 1 ½ cups BBQ sauce
- 1 cup carrots, thinly sliced
- 1 cup parsnips, thinly sliced
- 3 cloves garlic, peeled and crushed
- 1 pound pork ribs
- 1 cup leeks, thinly sliced
- 1/2 teaspoon ground black pepper
- 1/2 teaspoon salt

Directions

1. Arrange the ribs in the Instant Pot. Pour in the water and 1 cup of BBQ sauce. Close the cooker's lid. Choose the "Meat" key; cook for 25 minutes.
2. Add the leeks, parsnips, carrots, and garlic. Sprinkle with salt and ground black pepper. Cover, and select "Manual" function; set the timer for 5 minutes more.
3. Drizzle with the remaining ½ cup BBQ sauce and serve warm.

– PORK –

50. Festive Pot Roast

In this recipe, you will achieve a puffy crunchy crackling and juicy meat by using your electric pressure cooker. Go gourmet with this pork recipe by adding exotic spices like Wasabi powder, Ajowan seeds, Berbere seasoning, and so forth. Enjoy!

Servings 8

Ready in about
1 hour 15 minutes

NUTRITIONAL
INFORMATION
(Per Serving)

347 - Calories
14.1g - Fat
1.0g - Carbs
54.0g - Protein
0.0g - Sugars

Ingredients

- 2 tablespoons olive oil
- 1 bay leaf
- 2 cups beef broth
- 1/2 cup onion, chopped
- 1/4 teaspoon ground black pepper, to taste
- 1 teaspoon salt
- 3 pounds rump roast

Directions

1. Pat the rump roast dry and season with salt and black pepper.
2. Heat the oil in the cooking pot and select "Sauté" on the Instant Pot. Then, brown the meat on both sides for 10 minutes.
3. Remove your roast from the pot; add the onions, beef broth, and bay leaves; add the water to cover the ingredients. Add the roast back to the cooking pot.
4. Select HIGH pressure and 1 hour 5 minutes cook time. Remove prepared roast to a serving platter.
5. You can thicken the juices in the cooking pot with a slurry of water and cornstarch.

— PORK —

51. Comforting Potato and Bacon Soup

This potato soup might earn a permanent spot in your next menu planning simply because it is so delicious and easy to make. When blending, add a bit more milk to get your desired consistency.

Servings 6

Ready in about 15 minutes

NUTRITIONAL INFORMATION
(Per Serving)

409 - Calories
20.4g - Fat
35.5g - Carbs
20.9g - Protein
9.2g - Sugars

Ingredients

- 3 cups vegetable broth
- 1 tablespoon olive oil
- 4 slices bacon
- 1/2 pound carrots, diced
- 2 pounds potatoes, peeled and cubed
- 1 cup yellow onions, peeled and diced
- 1 cup canned evaporated milk
- 1 ½ cups water
- 1 tablespoon dried basil
- 1 teaspoon dried dill weed
- 1 teaspoon dried oregano
- 1 ½ teaspoons garlic powder
- 1/4 teaspoon ground black pepper
- 1 ½ teaspoons cayenne pepper
- 1 teaspoon salt

Directions

1. Press "Sauté" function and stir in the onion, bacon, and olive oil. Sauté for about 5 minutes, stirring continuously.
2. Add the vegetable broth, potatoes, carrots, and the seasonings. Stir to combine. Cover with the lid, press the "Steam" button and adjust the timer to 11 minutes.
3. When it beeps, perform a quick pressure release. Remove the bacon and reserve. Add water, evaporated milk, salt, and black pepper.
4. Mix with your immersion blender, but leave the chunks of potatoes. Taste and adjust the seasonings. Serve with reserved bacon.

– PORK –

52. Old-Fashioned Cassoulet

There are many recipes for the classic French cassoulet, but this is one of the tastiest that you have ever tried. You can thicken the cooking liquid by making the slurry with cornstarch and cold water as needed.

Servings 6

Ready in about 35 minutes

NUTRITIONAL INFORMATION (Per Serving)

447 - Calories
18.1g - Fat
12.6g - Carbs
55.9g - Protein
2.1g - Sugars

Ingredients

- 2 ½ pounds pork, cut into chunks
- 1 ¼ cups vegetable broth
- 1 ½ cups beans
- 2 ½ tablespoons canola oil
- 3 cloves garlic, finely minced
- 1/2 cup onion, diced
- 2 celery stalks, chopped
- 1/2 cup parsnip, chopped
- 1/2 cup carrots, chopped
- 1/2 teaspoon fennel seeds
- 2 sprigs dried thyme
- 1/2 teaspoon ground black pepper, to your liking
- 1/2 teaspoon cumin seeds
- 1 teaspoon salt
- 3/4 cup cheese, crumbled
- 1 ½ cups croutons

Directions

1. In a skillet, heat the canola oil; brown the pork chunks on all sides; season with salt and ground black pepper.
2. Place the pork into the Instant Pot and add the rest of the ingredients, except for the cheese. Seal the cooker's lid. Next, choose the "Stew" setting for 40 minutes.
3. Divide your cassoulet among individual bowls, and serve topped with cheese.

– PORK –

53. Spiced Chinese Ribs

If you're short on time, prepare Chinese ribs in your Instant pot and delight your family! Try adding a touch of hot paprika for extra flavor.

Servings 4

Ready in about 25 minutes

NUTRITIONAL INFORMATION
(Per Serving)

515 - Calories
20.8g - Fat
73.7g - Carbs
60.2g - Protein
17.6g - Sugars

Ingredients
- 1/4 cup olive oil
- 2 pounds pork ribs
- 3 ½ cups water
- 1 teaspoon salt
- 1 teaspoon cumin seeds
- 1 teaspoon garlic powder
- 1/3 teaspoon ground black pepper
- 1 teaspoon dried rosemary
- 1 ½ teaspoons onion powder
- 3 tablespoons brown sugar
- 1/2 cup ketchup
- 1 tablespoon Worcestershire sauce
- 12 cup wine vinegar

Directions
1. Mix the onion powder, garlic powder, ground black pepper, salt, rosemary and cumin seeds in a re-sealable plastic bag. Add the pork ribs to the bag; seal the bag and shake thoroughly until your ribs are completely coated.
2. Heat the olive oil in a wok or a wide saucepan over medium-high heat. Brown the ribs in hot oil for about 5 minutes per side.
3. Stir the water, ketchup, brown sugar, wine vinegar, and Worcestershire sauce in the pressure cooker. Add the browned ribs to the pressure cooker.
4. Lock the lid onto the pressure cooker. Then, reduce the heat to MEDIUM.
5. Cook the ribs for 20 minutes. Remove from heat and release pressure. Serve hot.

– PORK –

54. Penne with Sausage and Tomato Sauce

This classic pasta recipe has a slight twist and calls for shallots and bacon. Try adding freshly grated Parmesan cheese.

Servings 6

Ready in about 15 minutes

NUTRITIONAL INFORMATION
(Per Serving)

519 - Calories
21.5g - Fat
39.0g - Carbs
27.5g - Protein
1.3g - Sugars

Ingredients

- 1/2 pound sausage meat
- 3 cloves garlic, minced
- 1 cup shallot, finely chopped
- 1/2 pound bacon
- 1 ½ teaspoons dried oregano
- 1/2 teaspoon salt, or more to taste
- 1 tablespoon dried basil
- 2 cups penne pasta
- 1 ½ cups tomato purée
- 1/2 cup Parmesan cheese, grated

Directions

1. Set the cooker to "Sauté". Cook the bacon for about 5 minutes. Now brown the sausage until it's thoroughly cooked.
2. Add the shallot and garlic; sauté them for 5 minutes or until tender. Add the rest of the ingredients, except for the Parmesan cheese.
3. Choose "Manual" and LOW pressure for 6 minutes. Stir in the Parmesan cheese and serve right away. Bon appétit!

– PORK –

55. Spanish Chorizo and Garbanzo Beans with Escarole

You can experiment with seasonings in this recipe because it is hard to fail! Here are some ideas: mustard seeds, rosemary, seasoned salt, garlic pepper, ground allspice, etc. The possibilities are endless!

Servings 8

Ready in about 1 hour 5 minutes

NUTRITIONAL INFORMATION
(Per Serving)

351 - Calories
16.7g - Fat
34.6g - Carbs
17.1g - Protein
6.8g - Sugars

Ingredients

- 8 ounces Spanish chorizo, diced
- 2 cups garbanzo beans, dried
- 5 cups escarole, chopped
- 1 teaspoon kosher salt
- 1 bay leaf
- 1/4 cup sherry vinegar
- 1/2 teaspoon freshly ground black pepper
- 2 cups chicken broth
- 3 tablespoons olive oil
- 3 garlic cloves, minced
- 2 medium-sized onions, chopped
- 3 cups water

Directions

1. Heat the Instant Pot over medium-high heat and add the oil. Sauté the onion for 5 minutes. Stir in the garlic and chorizo and cook until aromatic.
2. Add the water, broth, garbanzo beans, and bay leaves. Close the lid securely and bring to HIGH pressure over high heat. Now, cook for 55 minutes.
3. Remove from the heat and release the pressure through a steam vent. Add the remaining ingredients and serve.

BEEF

– BEEF –

56. Country Beef Hash

Beef hash is one of the famous one-pot meals that cooks perfectly in the Instant Pot. Corned beef and potatoes combine very well and this meal is attractive in appearance, too.

Servings 6

Ready in about 20 minutes

NUTRITIONAL INFORMATION
(Per Serving)

340 - Calories
12.2g - Fat
15.4g - Carbs
31.9g - Protein
3.4g - Sugars

Ingredients

- 1/3 cup chicken broth
- 2 ½ tablespoons butter
- 2 red bell peppers, sliced
- 3 cloves garlic, minced
- 1/2 cup leek, chopped
- 1 ¼ pounds potatoes, diced
- 1 ½ pounds cooked deli corned beef, diced
- 1 teaspoon celery seeds
- 1/2 teaspoon ground black pepper, or more to taste
- 1 teaspoon salt
- 1 teaspoon fennel seeds

Directions

1. Melt the butter in the cooker turned to the Sauté function. Sauté the leeks, stirring often, until softened. Add the corned beef and garlic and cook for 5 minutes longer.
2. Stir in the remaining ingredients; stir until everything is well combined. Lock the lid onto the pot.
3. Cook for 14 minutes under HIGH pressure. Afterwards, use the quick-release function. Serve warm.

– BEEF –

57. Beef and Green Bean Soup

This soup is best enjoyed warm and it also has the advantage of being simple to prepare. Green beans make an excellent addition to this classic beef soup.

Servings 6

Ready in about 20 minutes

NUTRITIONAL INFORMATION (Per Serving)

353 - Calories
8.7g - Fat
27.0g - Carbs
42.1g - Protein
9.8g - Sugars

Ingredients

- 20 ounces green beans, trimmed and cut into small pieces
- 3 medium parsnips, finely chopped
- 2 onions, chopped
- 4 cloves garlic, minced
- 25 ounces canned tomatoes, diced
- 1 ½ pounds boneless beef bottom round, diced
- 1 cup carrots, diced
- 4 ½ cups beef broth
- 1/3 teaspoon ground black pepper
- 1 teaspoon salt
- 1 teaspoon dried marjoram

Directions

1. First, combine the broth, tomatoes, beef, garlic, onion, parsnip, carrots, marjoram, salt, and black pepper in a cooker. Lock the lid onto the pot.
2. Cook for 16 minutes under HIGH pressure. Use the quick-release method to drop the pressure.
3. Unlock and open the pot. Stir in the green beans. Then, seal the lid and wait for 4 minutes to warm up and blanch the beans. Serve hot with croutons of choice.

– BEEF –

58. Soft Vegetable Pot Roast

This meat and vegetable dish can help you find a balance between indulgence and nutrition. Root vegetables are a great source of vitamin C, vitamin A, magnesium, potassium, and dietary fiber.

Servings 8

Ready in about 40 minutes

NUTRITIONAL INFORMATION
(Per Serving)

418 - Calories
14.6g - Fat
17.8g - Carbs
48.8g - Protein
3.1g - Sugars

Ingredients

- 1 cup onions, thinly sliced
- 1 teaspoon dried marjoram
- 1/2 teaspoon ground black pepper, or more to taste
- 1/2 teaspoon garlic powder
- 1 teaspoon salt
- 1/2 teaspoon cayenne pepper
- 2 tablespoons tomato paste
- 1 ½ tablespoons canola oil
- 1 cup celery stalks, thinly sliced
- 2 ½ pounds chuck roast
- 1 ½ pounds potatoes, peeled and diced
- 1 cup carrots, peeled and thinly sliced
- 1/2 cup red wine
- 1 ¼ cups vegetable stock

Directions

1. Season the chuck roast with cayenne pepper, marjoram, garlic powder, salt and ground black pepper.
2. Place the inner pot in your cooker. Place canola oil in the inner pot. Press the "Meat" button. Sear the beef on all sides for 4 minutes. Reserve the beef.
3. Add the remaining ingredients to the inner pot; cook for 4 more minutes. Add the beef back to the pot.
4. Choose the "Keep Warm" function and cook for 32 minutes. Carefully remove the lid. Serve.

– BEEF –

59. Peasant Tomato Cabbage Rolls

Cabbage rolls are a staple winter dish. They also make an excellent addition to every holiday feast.

Servings 6

Ready in about 55 minutes

NUTRITIONAL
INFORMATION
(Per Serving)

454 - Calories
6.7g - Fat
61.3g - Carbs
35.6g - Protein
7.5g - Sugars

Ingredients

- 10 large cabbage leaves, blanched
- 1 ¼ pounds ground beef
- 4 cloves garlic, minced
- 1 cup onions, chopped
- 15 ounces canned tomato sauce
- 1/2 teaspoon paprika
- 1/2 teaspoon ground black pepper, to taste
- 1 teaspoon sea salt
- 2 cups rice
- 22 ounces canned diced tomatoes

Directions

1. Combine the onion, garlic, ground beef, rice, tomato sauce, salt, black pepper, and paprika in a mixing bowl; mix until everything is well combined.
2. Divide the meat mixture among blanched cabbage leaves. Roll the cabbage leaves up to form logs.
3. Stack the rolls in a cooker. Add the diced tomatoes.
4. Then, seal the cooker's lid. Now, cook for 55 minutes under LOW pressure. Use the quick-release function. Serve warm.

– BEEF –

60. Beef Brisket with Tomatillo Sauce

There are several ways to eat this amazing beef dish. You can make this flavorsome dish the day before and reheat to serve. For leftover sandwiches, just add a piquant mustard and a few pickles.

Servings 6

Ready in about 1 hour 15 minutes

NUTRITIONAL INFORMATION
(Per Serving)

350 - Calories
12.8g - Fat
9.8g - Carbs
47.7g - Protein
2.6g - Sugars

Ingredients

- 1 (2-pound) beef brisket
- 1 ¼ cups water
- 20 ounces canned whole tomatillos, drained
- 10 ounces canned chipotle peppers in adobo sauce
- 1 tablespoon olive oil
- 1 ¼ cups tomato sauce
- 4 cloves garlic, chopped
- 1/2 cup onion, chopped
- 1/2 teaspoon black pepper, to taste
- 1 teaspoon sea salt

Directions

1. Place the tomato sauce, tomatillos, chipotle peppers, water, salt, and black pepper in the bowl of a food processor; blend until smooth.
2. Heat the olive oil in your Instant Pot over medium heat; then, sauté the onion and garlic for about 4 minutes. Add the beef brisket to the cooker; sear it on all sides.
3. Pour the reserved tomatillo mixture over the brisket; bring to a boil. Cover with the lid and cook for 1 hour and 10 minutes.
4. Allow the cooker to release the pressure naturally. Serve with tomatillo sauce on the side.

– BEEF –

61. Short Ribs with Pearl Onions and Potatoes

If you don't like to peel pearl onions, here is a little trick: Allow them to boil for about 2 minutes in a saucepan; drain the onions using a colander and transfer them to an ice bath; cut off the root end; afterwards, squeeze each onion with your fingers and they will easily pop out of their skin.

In this recipe, you can substitute pearl onions for cipollini or shallots. A little dry wine is a nice touch to add.

Servings 8

Ready in about 45 minutes

NUTRITIONAL INFORMATION
(Per Serving)

424 - Calories
12.8g - Fat
36.4g - Carbs
39.2g - Protein
3.8g - Sugars

Ingredients

- 3 tablespoons olive oil
- 2 pounds short ribs, excess fat trimmed
- 1 bay leaf
- 1 ½ cups beef broth
- 2 tablespoons dry red wine
- 1 ½ cups water
- 2 cups pearl onions
- 8 medium-sized potatoes, quartered
- 2 sprigs rosemary
- 1/2 teaspoon freshly cracked black pepper, to taste
- 1 teaspoon salt

Directions

1. Coat the short ribs with salt and black pepper. Warm the oil in the inner pot. Choose the "Meat" mode. Brown the ribs on all sides. Set aside.
2. Add the pearl onions and sauté them for 6 minutes, until just tender.
3. Add the reserved ribs back to the pot; stir in the remaining ingredients. Press the "Stew" button and cook for 37-38 minutes.
4. Afterwards, carefully remove the lid. Serve at once.

– BEEF –

62. Old-fashioned Rich Stew

A hint of cumin powder adds a delicate flavor to this hearty beef stew. With crusty homemade bread, this stew turns into a two-course meal. Enjoy!

Servings 8

Ready in about 40 minutes

NUTRITIONAL INFORMATION
(Per Serving)

371 - Calories
7.3g - Fat
70.1g - Carbs
10.9g - Protein
2.2g - Sugars

Ingredients

- 2 tablespoons vegetable oil
- 1 bell pepper, seeded and coarsely chopped
- 3 garlic cloves, minced
- 1 cup red onion, chopped
- 20 ounces stew meat
- 3 tablespoons tomato paste
- 2 ½ cups beef bone broth
- 1/2 teaspoon black pepper, ground
- 1 teaspoon sea salt
- 1 cup carrots, chopped
- 6 small-sized potatoes, chopped
- 1/2 cup celery, chopped
- 1/2 teaspoon fennel seeds
- 1 bay leaf
- 1/2 teaspoon cumin powder
- 1/2 teaspoon red pepper flakes, crushed
- 2 ½ tablespoons arrowroot flour

Directions

1. Press the "Sauté" button on your Instant Pot. Now, sauté the meat, onion and garlic until the meat is no longer pink, about 6 minutes.
2. Add the other ingredients, except for arrowroot flour. Cover and press "Meat/ Stew" button.
3. Cook for 35 minutes under HIGH pressure.
4. To make the slurry, whisk 1/3 of the cooking liquid with the arrowroot flour. Add the slurry back to the pot. Serve immediately.

– BEEF –

63. Italian-Style Beef Soup

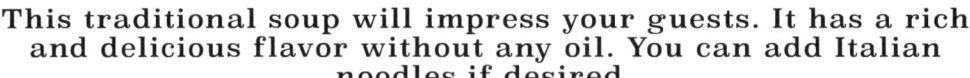

This traditional soup will impress your guests. It has a rich and delicious flavor without any oil. You can add Italian noodles if desired.

Servings 4

Ready in about 30 minutes

NUTRITIONAL INFORMATION
(Per Serving)

466 - Calories
10.6g - Fat
38.4g - Carbs
52.6g - Protein
8.1g - Sugars

Ingredients

- 4 cups beef broth
- 1 ¼ pounds ground beef
- 3 potatoes, diced
- 1 teaspoon minced garlic
- 1 cup onions, chopped
- 1 ½ cups cooked beans
- 2 ripe tomatoes, crushed
- 1/2 cup turnip, finely chopped
- 1/2 cup celery, finely chopped
- 1 cup carrots, trimmed and thinly sliced
- 1/2 teaspoon freshly ground black pepper
- 1 teaspoon salt

Directions

1. Add all of the above ingredients to your Instant Pot; give it a good stir.
2. Seal the lid according to manufacturer's directions; choose "Manual" mode and HIGH pressure for 25 minutes. Serve hot and enjoy.

– BEEF –

64. Traditional Beef Stroganoff

Classic beef Stroganoff is an all-time family favorite. In this recipe, bone-in short rib and chuck will work, too. Add 1 tablespoon of brandy for extra flavor.

Servings 6

Ready in about 25 minutes

NUTRITIONAL INFORMATION (Per Serving)

377 - Calories
16.9g - Fat
4.9g - Carbs
49.8g - Protein
2.1g - Sugars

Ingredients

- 2 cups beef stock
- 2 pounds beef sirloin, sliced
- 1 pound mushrooms, sliced
- 1 teaspoon fennel seeds
- 3 tablespoons vegetable oil
- 2 cloves garlic, peeled and crushed
- 1 onion, peeled and finely chopped
- 2 bay leaves
- 1 teaspoon dried thyme
- 1/2 teaspoon dried rosemary
- 1/4 cup Mozzarella cheese

Directions

1. Choose the "Meat" functions. Warm the oil in the cooker; sear the beef for 5 minutes.
2. Add the rest of the ingredients, except the cheese.
3. Place the lid on the pot; lock the lid. Push the "Stew" key and cook for 20 minutes. When the steam is completely released, carefully open the lid.

– BEEF –

65. Old-Fashioned Minestrone Soup

There is nothing more uplifting than the smell of a kitchen where old-fashioned soup is being made. Cooked beans are one of the simplest but the most delicious ways to enrich your soup.

Servings 4

Ready in about 30 minutes

NUTRITIONAL INFORMATION (Per Serving)

443 - Calories
10.7g - Fat
33.0g - Carbs
52.5g - Protein
9.7g - Sugars

Ingredients

- 1 ¼ cups cooked beans
- 1 quart beef broth
- 25 ounces canned tomatoes, crushed
- 1 cup carrots, trimmed and thinly sliced
- 2 potatoes, diced
- 1/2 celery stalks, chopped
- 2 cloves garlic, minced
- 1 cup onions, chopped
- 1 ¼ pounds ground beef
- 1/4 teaspoon ground black pepper
- 1/2 teaspoon sea salt

Directions

1. Add the ingredients to your Instant Pot and stir to combine.
2. Put the lid on; choose "Manual" and HIGH pressure for 25 minutes. Serve warm and enjoy.

– BEEF –

66. Herby Pasta with Meat and Mushrooms

With canned mushrooms and mixed ground meat combined with aromatic spices and herbs, this pasta dish is a crave-worthy combination.

Servings 4

Ready in about 25 minutes

NUTRITIONAL INFORMATION (Per Serving)

666 - Calories
12.7g - Fat
73.2g - Carbs
57.4g - Protein
6.3g - Sugars

Ingredients

- 1 ½ tablespoons canola oil
- 1 (4-ounce) can mushrooms, sliced
- 3/4 pound ground beef
- 1/2 pound ground pork
- 1/2 (24-ounce) jar pasta sauce
- 1/2 teaspoon dried sage
- 1/2 teaspoon sea salt
- 1/4 teaspoon ground black pepper
- 1 teaspoon dried dill weed
- 1 cup onions, chopped fine
- 3 cloves garlic, minced
- 1 teaspoon dried basil
- 1 teaspoon red pepper flakes
- 1 packet uncooked pasta
- 1 quart chicken broth
- 1/2 cup dry wine

Directions

1. Press the "Sauté" button and warm the canola oil. Sauté the garlic, onion, pork, and beef until browned, about 5 minutes.
2. Add the remaining ingredients. Stir until everything is well blended. Seal the cooker's lid and cook for 22-23 minutes. Release the pressure manually.
3. Serve with Mozzarella cheese if desired. Enjoy!

– BEEF –

67. Orange Short Ribs

Need a last-minute dish for a family Sunday dinner? Serve these sticky short ribs with a zesty flavor of blood orange

Servings 4

Ready in about 40 minutes

NUTRITIONAL INFORMATION
(Per Serving)

320 - Calories
13.8g - Fat
10.5g - Carbs
37.6g - Protein
3.7g - Sugars

Ingredients

- 3/4 cup water
- 1 cup soy sauce
- 2 tablespoons sweetener
- 1/2 cup blood orange, squeezed
- 1/2 head of garlic, peeled and crushed
- 3/4 cup scallions, chopped
- 1 teaspoon salt
- 1/2 teaspoon ground black pepper
- 1 pound beef short ribs
- 1 tablespoon sesame oil

Directions

1. Combine together the water, soy sauce, sweetener, and orange juice in a mixing bowl.
2. Add the garlic, scallions, salt, and ground black pepper; mix thoroughly. Place the ribs in the bowl and let them marinate at least 3 hours.
3. Heat sesame oil in a large skillet. Sear your ribs for about 4 minutes on each side. Transfer the seared short ribs to the Instant Pot.
4. Next, choose the "Meat\Stew" mode, and cook for 35 minutes. To release pressure, use natural release method. Serve warm.

– BEEF –

68. Pulled BBQ Beef

If you have friends coming over, these sandwiches should be on the menu! Serve with lots of salad. Enjoy!

Servings 6

Ready in about 1 hour 5 minutes

NUTRITIONAL INFORMATION (Per Serving)

239 - Calories
7.3g - Fat
6.4g - Carbs
35.4g - Protein
5.9g - Sugars

Ingredients

- Non-stick cooking spray
- 1 ½ cups beef stock
- 1 ½ pounds frozen beef roast

For the BBQ sauce:
- 1/3 cup water
- 1/3 cup ketchup
- 1/4 teaspoon ground black pepper
- 1/2 teaspoon kosher salt
- 1/2 teaspoon paprika
- 1 tablespoon honey

Directions

1. Lightly oil your Instant Pot with a cooking spray. Put beef roast and stock into the pot. Put the lid on, choose the "Meat" key and set to 1 hour 5 minutes.
2. Meanwhile, combine together the BBQ sauce ingredients in a mixing bowl.
3. Turn the pot off. Next, use a quick pressure release. Now, pull the cooked meat apart into the chunks.
4. Add the beef back to the Instant Pot; pour the BBQ sauce over it. Assemble the sandwiches and serve.

– BEEF –

69. Herbed Mustard Roast

Make this aromatic, juicy roast when you want to surprise your family with something new and tasty. In addition, rump roast is less expensive cut of meat. Win-win!

Servings 6

Ready in about 1 hour 5 minutes

NUTRITIONAL INFORMATION
(Per Serving)

443 - Calories
16.5g - Fat
1.2g - Carbs
72.2g - Protein
0.0g - Sugars

Ingredients

- 1 tablespoon olive oil
- 2 cups beef broth
- 1 ½ teaspoons Dijon mustard
- 1/2 cup scallions, chopped
- 3 pounds rump roast
- 1 teaspoon salt
- 1/2 teaspoon cayenne pepper
- 1/4 teaspoon freshly cracked black pepper
- 1 bay leaf
- 1/2 teaspoon dried marjoram, crushed
- 2 sprigs dried rosemary, crushed

Directions

1. Pat the rump roast dry and rub with rosemary, marjoram, Dijon mustard, salt, black pepper, and cayenne pepper.
2. Warm the olive oil in the cooking pot and select "Sauté" on the Instant Pot. Then, brown the meat on both sides.
3. Remove your roast from the pot; add the scallions, beef broth, and bay leaves; add the water to cover the ingredients. Add the roast back to the cooking pot.
4. Select HIGH pressure and 1 hour 5minutes cook time. Serve warm.

– BEEF –

70. Spaghetti with Bacon and Beef Sauce

Loaded with ground beef, bacon, and pasta sauce this spaghetti recipe is just as good with your family dinner, as it is served on a special occasion.

Servings 6

Ready in about 15 minutes

NUTRITIONAL INFORMATION
(Per Serving)

462 - Calories
18.4g - Fat
49.6g - Carbs
32.6g - Protein
7.9g - Sugars

Ingredients

- 1/2 tablespoon butter, softened
- 3 slices bacon, chopped
- 1 pound ground beef
- 1/2 teaspoon ground black pepper, to taste
- 1 teaspoon sea salt
- 1 cup onion, peeled and chopped
- 2 tablespoons olive oil
- 3 garlic cloves, peeled and crushed
- 1/2 teaspoon dried marjoram
- 1 teaspoon dried basil
- 1 ½ teaspoons Dijon mustard
- 1 ½ pounds pasta sauce
- 2 ½ cups dried spaghetti

Directions

1. Select the "Sauté" button; warm the olive oil and butter; sauté the onion, garlic, beef, and bacon, stirring frequently, until they are tender for about 6 minutes.
2. Add the remaining ingredients. Cook for 9 minutes. Serve at once.

– BEEF –

71. Hamburger Cabbage and Barley Soup

Make the best hamburger soup without spending too much time over the stove! Barley is a versatile whole grain that is high in fiber and other valuable nutrients. Actually, it is a quicker alternative to pearled barley.

Servings 6

Ready in about 25 minutes

NUTRITIONAL INFORMATION (Per Serving)

350 - Calories
8.7g - Fat
31.1g - Carbs
36.9g - Protein
6.3g - Sugars

Ingredients

- 5 cups beef stock
- 1/2 teaspoon freshly cracked black pepper
- 1 teaspoon sea salt
- 1 ½ cups Roma tomatoes, seeded and chopped
- 1 ½ pounds hamburger
- 1 ½ cups carrots, peeled and sliced
- 1 cup celery stalk, chopped
- 1 cup parsnips, sliced
- 1 cup red onion, finely chopped
- 3 garlic cloves, minced
- 4 cups cabbage, chopped
- 1 ½ teaspoons dried marjoram
- 1 sprig dried thyme
- 3/4 cup quick barley

Directions

1. Press the "Sauté" button and cook the hamburger for 5 minutes. Drain off the excess fat; stir in the garlic and onion; continue sautéing a few more minutes.
2. Next, add the beef stock, tomatoes, and barley. Choose the "Soup" function and let it cook under HIGH pressure for about 15 minutes.
3. Perform a quick pressure release; add the rest of the ingredients. Put the cooker's lid back on and press the "Soup" button; bring to HIGH pressure for 5 minutes. Serve warm.

– BEEF –

72. Beef and Yogurt Curry

This rich and flavorful curry is sure to please because it simply melts in your mouth. You can use frozen vegetables because they're much more economical! Why? Because you don't pay for pits, stalks, and rind – just 100 percent edible parts of vegetables!

Servings 4

Ready in about 30 minutes

NUTRITIONAL INFORMATION
(Per Serving)

279 - Calories
8.1g - Fat
16.7g - Carbs
31.7g - Protein
8.8g - Sugars

Ingredients

- 1 cup zucchini, peeled and diced
- 1 ½ tablespoons vinegar
- A pinch of cinnamon powder
- 1/2 teaspoon ground allspice
- 1 ½ cups beef stock
- 1/2 cup onion, chopped
- 1/2 cup parsnip, chopped
- 1 cup carrot, chopped
- 3 cloves garlic, peeled and minced
- 1 cup turnip, peeled and chopped
- 1 ½ tablespoons red curry paste
- 3/4 pound beef, cut into pieces
- 1/2 teaspoon black pepper, to your liking
- 1 teaspoon salt
- 1 cup natural yogurt

Directions

1. Simply place all the ingredients, except for yogurt, into your Instant Pot.
2. Cover with the lid and press the "Meat" button; cook for 30 minutes.
3. While the curry is still hot, pour in natural yogurt. Stir until everything is well combined.
4. Serve over rice. Enjoy!

– BEEF –

73. Beef and Kale Stew with Noodles

What could be better than a beef stew with root vegetables? Yummy beef stew with root vegetables, greens and lots of goodies mixed in!

Servings 8

Ready in about 27 minutes

NUTRITIONAL INFORMATION (Per Serving)

265 - Calories
10.0g - Fat
16.4g - Carbs
24.5g - Protein
3.7g - Sugars

Ingredients

- 3 tablespoons butter
- 1 cup onions, diced
- 1 ½ cups carrots, diced
- 1 teaspoon dried thyme
- 1 teaspoon cayenne pepper
- 1/4 teaspoon black pepper, to taste
- 1/2 teaspoon salt
- 1 ½ teaspoons dried basil leaves
- 1 teaspoon marjoram
- 2 cups Roma tomatoes, seeded and chopped
- 1 cup kale, chopped
- 7 ½ cups bone broth
- 1 pound ground beef
- 1/3 cup white wine
- 10 ounces noodles

Directions

1. Set your cooker to "Sauté". Now, melt the butter; then, add the ground beef and all of the seasonings. Cook until the meat has become brown (about 5 minutes).
2. Add the onions and carrot, and cook for about 6 minutes. Pour in the wine to deglaze the pan.
3. Add the rest of the ingredients and stir to combine. Set the cooker to 14 minutes. Serve topped with fresh cilantro if desired.

– BEEF –

74. Holiday Short Ribs

Firstly, brown the ribs to seal the natural juices and flavors before starting pressure cooking. Add small potatoes and fresh herbs, and turn ordinary short ribs into something spectacular!

Servings 8

Ready in about 45 minutes

NUTRITIONAL INFORMATION (Per Serving)

388 - Calories
12.5g - Fat
29.3g - Carbs
37.6g - Protein
3.6g - Sugars

Ingredients

- 3 tablespoons vegetable oil
- 3 cloves garlic, peeled and crushed
- 1 cup onions, chopped
- 6 potatoes, small
- 1 teaspoon salt
- 1 ½ teaspoons cayenne pepper
- 1/2 teaspoon black pepper, to taste
- 2 pounds short ribs, excess fat trimmed
- 2 sprigs thyme
- 2 sprigs rosemary
- 2 bay leaves
- 1 ½ cups carrots, peeled and thinly sliced
- 2 tablespoons dry red wine
- 1 ¼ cups vegetable stock
- 1 ¼ cups water

Directions

1. Season generously the short ribs with cayenne pepper, salt, and black pepper. Warm vegetable oil in the inner pot. Select the "Meat" function. Now brown the ribs on all sides. Set aside.
2. Add the carrots, garlic, and onion, and sauté for 7 minutes.
3. Add the reserved ribs back to the pot; stir in the remaining ingredients. Press the "Stew" key and cook for 38 minutes.
4. Afterwards, carefully remove the lid. Serve warm.

— BEEF —

75. BBQ Beef Sandwiches

Select a great beef roast and make these rich and satisfying sandwiches for your family. With a great homemade sauce, these sandwiches are addictive!

Servings 6

Ready in about
1 hour 5 minutes

NUTRITIONAL
INFORMATION
(Per Serving)

265 - Calories
7.4g - Fat
13.2g - Carbs
35.8g - Protein
12.0g - Sugars

Ingredients

- 1 ½ cups beef stock
- 1 ½ pounds frozen beef roast

For the BBQ sauce:
- 1 tablespoon honey
- 2 tablespoons water
- 1/2 teaspoon ground black pepper
- 1 teaspoon salt
- 1/2 teaspoon cayenne pepper
- 1 cup ketchup

Directions

1. Grease the Instant Pot with a nonstick cooking spray. Drop beef roast and stock into the pot. Put the lid on and select the "Meat" button; adjust the time to 1 hour 5 minutes.
2. In the meantime, combine the BBQ sauce ingredients thoroughly. Turn the pot off.
3. Use a quick pressure release. Then, pull the cooked meat apart into chunks.
4. Add the beef back to the Instant Pot; pour the BBQ sauce over the meat. Assemble the sandwiches and serve.

FISH & SEAFOOD

— FISH & SEAFOOD —

76. Tuna Salad with Noodles and Mozzarella

Tuna salad is a must-have during the summer season. With this recipe, you can turn this evergreen recipe into something fantastic, adding carefully selected seasonings and freshly grated mellow cheese.

Servings 6

Ready in about 18 minutes

NUTRITIONAL INFORMATION (Per Serving)

204 - Calories
8.6g - Fat
17.6g - Carbs
14.5g - Protein
2.9g - Sugars

Ingredients

- 1 ½ cups tuna fish in water, drained
- 1 ½ tablespoons olive oil
- 1 ½ cups water
- 1/2 teaspoon black pepper
- 1/4 teaspoon red pepper flakes, crushed
- 1 teaspoon sea salt
- 1 teaspoon garlic powder
- 16 ounces canned tomatoes, diced
- 1 cup leeks, chopped
- 10 ounces dry egg noodles
- Mozzarella cheese, for garnish

Directions

1. Warm the olive oil over medium heat; sauté the leeks for about 4 minutes.
2. Stir in the noodles, tomatoes, and water; click the "Soup" button and set the timer to 10 minutes. Turn your Instant Pot off.
3. Add the rest of the ingredients, except the cheese; cook for 5 more minutes until it is warmed enough. Serve garnished with Mozzarella cheese.

— FISH & SEAFOOD —

77. Saucy Fish Fillets with Onion

There's more than one way to cook fish fillets. But, when you want to please your family, pressure cooked flaky and buttery fish fillets are a must.

Servings 4

Ready in about 12 minutes

NUTRITIONAL INFORMATION
(Per Serving)

256 - Calories
13.7g - Fat
6.7g - Carbs
26.4g - Protein
4.7g - Sugars

Ingredients

- 1/4 cup olive oil
- 1 tablespoon lemon juice
- 1 teaspoon lemon zest, grated
- 1 cup onions, cut into rings
- 1 ½ tablespoons brown sugar
- 1 pound white fish filets
- 1 teaspoon salt
- 1/2 teaspoon ground black pepper, to taste
- 1 teaspoon cayenne pepper
- 2 tablespoons fresh cilantro
- 2 tablespoons fresh parsley

Directions

1. Season the fish filets with cayenne pepper, salt and black pepper. Press the "Sauté" key and brown the filets on both sides, for about 5 minutes.
2. Add about 1 cup of water to the pot. Lay the browned fish fillets on the metal rack. Place the onion over the fish fillets. Seal the cooker's lid and choose "Steam" for about 7 minutes.
3. Meanwhile, whisk the remaining ingredients in a mixing bowl. Then, pour the sauce over the fish fillets and onion rings.

– FISH & SEAFOOD –

78. Creamy Fish Curry

White fish pairs perfectly with unsweetened coconut milk in this heavenly delicious and light curry. Serve with hot jasmine rice for an additional hint of the tropics!

Servings 6

Ready in about 13 minutes

NUTRITIONAL INFORMATION
(Per Serving)

371 - Calories
21.0g - Fat
6.6g - Carbs
38.3g - Protein
0.8g - Sugars

Ingredients

- 2 pounds white fish fillets, cut into bite-size pieces
- 1 ½ tablespoons fresh lemon juice
- 1/2 cup unsweetened coconut milk
- 1 teaspoon salt
- 1 bay leaf
- 1/2 teaspoon chili powder
- 1/2 teaspoon ginger powder
- 1 teaspoon ground turmeric
- 1/2 teaspoon ground cumin
- 2 garlic cloves, finely minced
- 1 cup shallot, chopped
- 2 tablespoons olive oil

Directions

1. Choose the "Sauté" function. Warm olive oil and sauté the shallot, garlic and ginger until they are softened, about 5 minutes. Add the chili powder, cumin, and turmeric.
2. Cook for 3 more minutes and add the rest of the ingredients, except for the lemon juice.
3. Cover and press "Manual"; choose 5-minute pressure cooking time. Drizzle with lemon juice and serve immediately.

— FISH & SEAFOOD —

79. Rice and Tuna Salad

This salad is so simple and quick to make and contains great flavors of petits pois (small green peas) and light tuna pieces.

Servings 4

Ready in about 25 minutes

NUTRITIONAL INFORMATION
(Per Serving)

490 - Calories
13.6g - Fat
57.9g - Carbs
32.5g - Protein
1.3g - Sugars

Ingredients

- 1 tablespoon extra-virgin olive oil
- 1/2 cup frozen petits pois, defrosted
- 1 cup onion, thinly sliced
- 1 ½ cups brown rice
- 3 cups water
- 1/2 teaspoon ground black pepper
- 1 teaspoon salt
- 1 teaspoon dried dill weed
- 1/2 teaspoon red pepper flakes
- 2 ½ cups tuna in spring water
- 1/2 cup flat-leaf parsley, roughly chopped

Directions

1. Add lightly salted water and rice to your cooker. Close and lock the lid. Choose "Manual" function and 24-minute pressure cooking time.
2. Then, open the cooker using natural pressure release. Allow your rice to cool completely.
3. Add the rest of the ingredients. Stir and serve well chilled.

– FISH & SEAFOOD –

80. Cod Fillets with Cremini Mushrooms

Cod fillets are a cinch to make in the Instant pot. With an addition of Cremini mushrooms, this is amazing, belly filling recipe.

Servings 4

Ready in about 13 minutes

NUTRITIONAL INFORMATION (Per Serving)

232 - Calories
12.4g - Fat
2.6g - Carbs
27.0g - Protein
0.8g - Sugars

Ingredients

- 1 pound cod fillets
- 2 tablespoons olive oil
- 1/2 tablespoon lemon juice
- 1 teaspoon salt
- 1/2 teaspoon ground black pepper, to taste
- 2 tablespoons fresh cilantro
- 2 tablespoons fresh parsley
- 1/2 tablespoon balsamic vinegar
- 1 ½ tablespoons butter, melted
- 1 teaspoon dried rosemary
- 1/2 cup green onions, coarsely chopped
- 1 ½ cups Cremini mushrooms, sliced

Directions

1. Drizzle the melted butter over the cod fillets. Then, coat the filets with dried rosemary, salt, and ground black pepper. Press the "Sauté" button and brown the fillets for 5 minutes.
2. Add about 1 cup water to the pot. Arrange the fish fillets on the metal rack. Place chopped green onion and mushrooms over the fish fillets.
3. Seal the cooker's lid and choose "Steam" for about 8 minutes.
4. To make the sauce, whisk the remaining ingredients in a mixing bowl. To serve, spoon the sauce over the fish fillets and mushrooms. Enjoy!

— FISH & SEAFOOD —

81. Salmon Fillets in Mayonnaise Sauce

This meal is so simple to make and contains rich flavors of Mediterranean herbs. Fresh-from-the-sea salmon fillets are a great family meal for any occasion.

Servings 4

Ready in about 9 minutes

NUTRITIONAL INFORMATION
(Per Serving)

211 - Calories
12.0g - Fat
3.9g - Carbs
22.3g - Protein
1.1g - Sugars

Ingredients

- 1/4 cup mayonnaise
- 2 tablespoons fresh lemon juice
- 1/2 teaspoon salt
- 1/2 teaspoon cayenne pepper
- 2 tablespoons fresh parsley
- 1/4 teaspoon ground black pepper, or more to taste
- 2 sprigs rosemary
- 2 sprigs thyme
- 1 pound salmon filets

Directions

1. Sprinkle the salmon filets with cayenne pepper, salt, and ground black pepper. Choose "Sauté" mode and brown your filets on all sides for 5 minutes.
2. Place the rack at the bottom of your cooker. Add about 1 cup of water to the pot. Lay the browned salmon fillets on the rack.
3. Seal the cooker's lid and select the "Steam" setting; cook for 4 minutes.
4. In the meantime, prepare the sauce. Mix the remaining ingredients in a mixing bowl. Then, pour the sauce over the filets.

— FISH & SEAFOOD —

82. Sausage and Seafood Delight

Here's a great addition to your holiday menu! This rich and flavorful meal is simply delicious; sausage, seafood and vegetables make a great blend.

Servings 6

Ready in about 15 minutes

NUTRITIONAL INFORMATION
(Per Serving)

509 - Calories
24.6g - Fat
23.4g - Carbs
38.0g - Protein
2.7g - Sugars

Ingredients

- 2 corn on the cobs, quartered
- 6 medium-sized potatoes, peeled and diced
- 16 clams
- 3 ½ cups water
- 1/2 teaspoon ground black pepper, or more to taste
- 1 teaspoon salt
- 3/4 cup vegetable stock
- 1 bay leaf
- 2 ½ pounds shrimp
- 1 ½ pounds smoked sausage, sliced
- 1 cup fresh chopped chives, as garnish

Directions

1. Simply place all the ingredients, except for chives, into the inner pot of your cooker.
2. Press the "Beans" button; cook for about 16 minutes. Serve sprinkled with chopped chives. Enjoy!

– FISH & SEAFOOD –

83. Tuna and Brown Rice Salad

This salad is especially loved by those on weight loss. Did you know that brown rice is a great source of fiber and other components that promote fat loss?

Servings 4

Ready in about 25 minutes

NUTRITIONAL INFORMATION (Per Serving)

442 - Calories
8.2g - Fat
64.5g - Carbs
26.8g - Protein
5.0g - Sugars

Ingredients

- 1 ½ cups light tuna in water
- 1 cup tomato, diced
- 1 ½ cups brown rice
- 3 cloves garlic, crushed
- 2 yellow onions, chopped
- 2 cups water
- 1/2 teaspoon black pepper, to taste
- 1 teaspoon salt
- 1 teaspoon dried dill weed
- 1/2 cup red bell pepper, seeded and thinly sliced
- 1/2 cup orange bell pepper, seeded and thinly sliced

Directions

1. Add the water and brown rice to your cooker. Close and lock the lid. Choose "Manual" setting and 24-minute pressure cooking time.
2. Then, use Natural pressure release method. Allow the rice to cool completely.
3. Stir in the remaining ingredients, stir, and serve chilled.

— FISH & SEAFOOD —

84. Tuna with Noodles and Feta

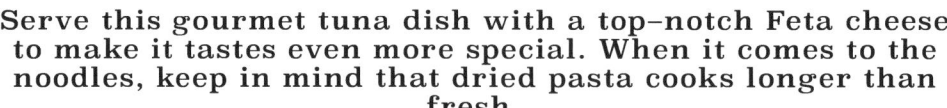

Serve this gourmet tuna dish with a top-notch Feta cheese to make it tastes even more special. When it comes to the noodles, keep in mind that dried pasta cooks longer than fresh.

Servings 6

Ready in about 17 minutes

NUTRITIONAL INFORMATION
(Per Serving)

199 - Calories
8.7g - Fat
17.1g - Carbs
13.2g - Protein
3.1g - Sugars

Ingredients

- 1 ½ cups tuna fish in water, drained
- 16 ounces canned tomatoes, diced
- 1 cup red onions, chopped
- 2 tablespoons vegetable oil
- 1/2 teaspoon black pepper
- 1 teaspoon sea salt
- 1 teaspoon garlic powder
- 1/2 teaspoon dried basil
- 1 ½ cups water
- 10 ounces dry egg noodles
- Feta cheese, crumbled

Directions

1. Warm the oil and sauté the onions for about 3 minutes.
2. Stir in the noodles, tomatoes, water; click the "Soup" button and set the timer to 9 minutes. Then turn the pot off.
3. Add the remaining ingredients, except for the Feta cheese; cook for 5 more minutes until it is warmed enough. Serve garnished with Feta cheese.

– FISH & SEAFOOD –

85. Saucy Salmon Fillets

This salmon dish has the aroma of the Mediterranean when you open the Instant pot. It can be served as a delicious everyday lunch or an elegant Sunday dinner.

Servings 6

Ready in about 12 minutes

NUTRITIONAL INFORMATION
(Per Serving)

323 - Calories
19.7g - Fat
8.5g - Carbs
29.5g - Protein
6.5g - Sugars

Ingredients

- 3 tablespoons olive oil
- 1 ½ tablespoons lemon juice
- 1/2 teaspoon ground black pepper, or more to taste
- 1 teaspoon salt
- 1/4 cup mayonnaise
- 12 teaspoons brown sugar
- 6 salmon filets
- 1/4 cup fresh parsley

Directions

1. Season the salmon filets with salt and black pepper. Press "Sauté" and brown your filets on both sides for about 6 minutes.
2. Add about 1 cup of water to the pot. Lay the browned salmon filets on the rack. Seal the cooker's lid and choose "Steam" for about 6 minutes.
3. In the meantime, mix the remaining ingredients in a bowl. Then, pour the sauce over the filets.

VEGAN

– VEGAN –

86. Homemade Pumpkin Purée

People often tend to think of pumpkin as little more than a pie filling. Actually, this orange plant has a lot of health benefits: it regulates blood pressure, improves eye health, boosts our immune system, fights free radicals, etc.

Servings 12

Ready in about 12 minutes

NUTRITIONAL
INFORMATION
(Per Serving)

145 - Calories
0.4g - Fat
37.2g - Carbs
1.7g - Protein
30.0g - Sugars

Ingredients

- 4 pounds pie pumpkins, stem removed, cut in half, and seeds removed
- 1 ½ cups sugar
- 2 ½ cups water

Directions

1. Place the steamer basket in your Instant Pot. Pour in the water.
2. Cut the pumpkin half into four pieces. Place the pumpkin in the steamer. Close and lock the lid. Set the burner heat to HIGH. Set the timer to cook for 12 minutes.
3. Then open the cooker with the Quick pressure release method.
4. Make sure not to overcook. When it is cool enough to handle, scoop the flesh from the peel using a soup spoon.
5. Process the pumpkin along with sugar using an immersion blender for about 2 minutes. Enjoy!

– VEGAN –

87. Romantic Apricot Oatmeal

Fruit oatmeal is a delicious and highly nutritious breakfast; it is especially recommended for diet conscious people.

Servings 2

Ready in about 14 minutes

NUTRITIONAL INFORMATION (Per Serving)

371 - Calories
24.0g - Fat
35.6g - Carbs
7.2g - Protein
11.5g - Sugars

Ingredients

- 3/4 cup almond milk
- 3/4 cup steel-cut oats
- 1 teaspoon coconut extract
- 1/2 teaspoon vanilla paste
- 5 apricots, pitted and halved
- A pinch of cinnamon powder
- 1 ½ cups water

Directions

1. Simply place all of the above ingredients in the inner pot.
2. Now, press the "Manual" button; set to 4 minutes.
3. Use the natural pressure release method according to the instructions. Serve warm and enjoy.

– VEGAN –

88. Basic Apple Sauce

Throw just three ingredients into your Instant pot and make one of the most popular multi-purpose sauces. What could be simpler? Use this basic apple sauce to make dessert, breakfast and snack recipes all year long.

Servings 16

Ready in about 10 minutes

NUTRITIONAL INFORMATION (Per Serving)

73 - Calories
0.2g - Fat
19.2g - Carbs
0.4g - Protein
14.5g - Sugars

Ingredients

- 1/3 cup water
- 10 apples, cored and diced
- 1/3 teaspoon cinnamon powder

Directions

1. Arrange the diced apples in the inner pot of your Instant Pot.
2. Add cinnamon and water. Place a circle of parchment paper over the apples. Cover and use "Manual" setting; then, set cooking time to 8 minutes.
3. Afterwards, release the pressure naturally. Mix with an immersion blender until smooth and creamy. Enjoy!

- VEGAN -

89. Morning Aromatic Congee

Fragrant jasmine rice with sweet onions and mirin, which is a popular ingredient in Japanese cuisine. This is a complete treat for your family and guests.

Servings 6

Ready in about 40 minutes

NUTRITIONAL INFORMATION (Per Serving)

240 - Calories
0.1g - Fat
55.0g - Carbs
4.3g - Protein
3.5g - Sugars

Ingredients

- 2 cups jasmine rice
- 1 teaspoon salt
- 1 teaspoon minced fresh ginger
- 1/4 cup mirin
- 2 garlic cloves, minced
- 1 cup sweet onions, finely chopped
- 8 cups water

Directions

1. Mix all the ingredients in your Instant Pot. Lock the lid onto the pot.
2. Set the machine to cook at HIGH pressure. Set the timer for 50 minutes. Reduce the pressure following the manufacturer's instructions.
3. Turn off the machine and let the pressure fall to normal. Afterwards, remove the lid. Serve warm.

– VEGAN –

90. Cilantro Breakfast Quinoa

Make this easy and healthy breakfast in no time. In this recipe, you can freely experiment with seasonings. Ground bay leaves, red pepper flakes, and turmeric powder work well too.

Servings 6

Ready in about 3 minutes

NUTRITIONAL INFORMATION
(Per Serving)

320 - Calories
10.2g - Fat
47.6g - Carbs
10.3g - Protein
0.8g - Sugars

Ingredients

- 2 ½ cups quinoa, well rinsed
- 1/4 teaspoon ground black pepper
- 1/2 teaspoon cayenne pepper
- 1/2 teaspoon salt
- 1/4 teaspoon allspice
- 2 ½ tablespoons olive oil
- 1 teaspoon minced garlic
- 1 cup onions, chopped
- 1/4 cup fresh cilantro, coarsely chopped

Directions

1. In the preheated Instant Pot, warm the olive oil until sizzling; sauté the onions and garlic for 2 minutes or until they become browned.
2. Tap the quinoa from the strainer into the cooker. Then, stir in the remaining ingredients, except the cilantro.
3. Close and lock the lid. Cook for 2 minutes at HIGH pressure. Fluff the prepared quinoa with a fork and garnish with fresh cilantro. Serve.

– VEGAN –

91. Potato and Porcini Mushroom Soup

You don't have to be a vegan to enjoy this ultimate comfort soup. It will keep you warm and hydrated. You can freeze the leftovers and reheat on windy days. Lovely!

Servings 10

Ready in about 15 minutes

NUTRITIONAL INFORMATION
(Per Serving)

96 - Calories
0.8g - Fat
19.5g - Carbs
3.3g - Protein
3.7g - Sugars

Ingredients

- 8 ½ cups water, boiling
- 1 ½ cups Porcini mushrooms, roughly chopped
- 1 cup carrots, peeled and diced
- 2 pounds potatoes, peeled and cubed
- 1/2 cup celery stalk, chopped
- 1/3 teaspoon marjoram
- 1/2 teaspoon black pepper, to your liking
- 1/2 teaspoon salt
- 1 teaspoon dried dill weed
- 3 cloves garlic, minced
- 1 cup yellow onions, sliced into rings
- 1 ½ cups non-dairy milk, unsweetened

Directions

1. Click the "Sauté" button; sauté the yellow onions and garlic for 6 minutes, adding a splash of water as needed.
2. Stir in the remaining ingredients, except for the milk. Cover and cook under HIGH pressure for about 7 minutes.
3. Open the lid following the manufacturer's directions. Pour in the milk.
4. Blend the soup in a food processor or use your hand blender for 3 minutes. Serve your soup topped with croutons if desired.

– VEGAN –

92. Kidney Bean Salad

This delicious salad with multiple layers of flavor is designed to satisfy you for hours. Kidney beans is a powerhouse of vegan protein, while the vegetables are packed with vitamins, minerals, and fiber.

Servings 4

Ready in about 20 minutes

NUTRITIONAL INFORMATION
(Per Serving)

313 - Calories
10.1g - Fat
44.0g - Carbs
14.4g - Protein
3.5g - Sugars

Ingredients

- 1 ¼ cups dry kidney beans, soaked
- 4 ½ cups water
- 3/4 cup shallots, chopped
- 2 sprigs thyme
- 2 sprigs rosemary
- 1/2 cup green bell pepper, thinly sliced
- 1 cup red bell pepper, thinly sliced
- 2 ½ tablespoons olive oil
- 2 tablespoons apple cider vinegar
- 1 ½ tablespoons sunflower seeds
- 1 teaspoon sea salt
- 1/2 teaspoon ground black pepper, or more to taste

Directions

1. Add the water, soaked kidney beans, shallots, thyme, and rosemary to the inner pot of your cooker.
2. Cover and press the "Manual" button, set the cooking time to 20 minutes.
3. Then, open your Instant Pot by using natural pressure release. Drain the cooked kidney beans and add the remaining ingredients. Serve well chilled.

– VEGAN –

93. Easy Key Lime Quinoa

Key lime can help you fight infections and slow down ageing. It also enhances the digestion and protects your heart.

Servings 6

Ready in about 7 minutes

NUTRITIONAL INFORMATION
(Per Serving)

164 - Calories
2.6g - Fat
30.0g - Carbs
6.2g - Protein
0.0g - Sugars

Ingredients

- 2 cups water
- 6 slices of key lime
- 1/2 teaspoon freshly cracked black pepper
- 1 teaspoon seasoned salt
- 1 ½ cups quinoa, rinsed well

Directions

1. In your cooker, place all of the above ingredients, except for the key lime slices.
2. Close and lock the lid. Select the "Manual" function and cook for 2 minutes. Next, open the cooker using Natural pressure release for 5 minutes.
3. Taste and adjust the seasonings. Serve with key lime slices.

– VEGAN –

94. Perfect Banana Barley Congee

Rice and grains are one of the healthiest foods in the world. In this recipe, we use an amazing mix of barley, brown rice and buckwheat. Barley is a great source of dietary fiber; brown rice has antioxidant benefits; buckwheat improves heart health and digestion.

Servings 4

Ready in about 30 minutes

NUTRITIONAL INFORMATION
(Per Serving)

404 - Calories
2.1g - Fat
88.8g - Carbs
9.2g - Protein
7.8g - Sugars

Ingredients

- 2 bananas, cubed
- 1 teaspoon vanilla extract
- 1/2 teaspoon ground cloves
- 1 cup pot barley
- 1 cup brown rice
- 1/2 cup buckwheat
- 1/2 teaspoon cinnamon powder
- 1/4 teaspoon kosher salt, or more to taste

Directions

1. Add all of the above ingredients to the inner pot of your Instant Pot. Pour in about 8 cups of water
2. Close the lid and choose "Porridge" mode; cook for 30 minutes.
3. Sweeten with agave nectar or maple syrup. Serve warm.

– VEGAN –

95. Old-fashioned Savory Rice Porridge

Porridge is such a versatile food! You can serve it as a vegan main course, everyday family dinner or a festive side dish.

Servings 6

Ready in about 50 minutes

NUTRITIONAL INFORMATION
(Per Serving)

237 - Calories
0.5g - Fat
52.0g - Carbs
5.0g - Protein
0.7g - Sugars

Ingredients

- 2 cups basmati rice
- 1 teaspoon paprika
- 1/2 teaspoon black pepper, ground
- 1 teaspoon salt
- 3 garlic cloves, minced
- 1 ½ cups scallions, finely chopped
- 8 cups water

Directions

1. Combine all of the above ingredients in your Instant Pot. Lock the lid onto the pot.
2. Click the "Rice" button and cook for 50 minutes. Reduce the pressure following the manufacturer's instructions.
3. Let the pressure fall to normal and remove the lid. Serve warm and enjoy.

– VEGAN –

96. Nutty Oatmeal with Dried Fruits

This simple but endlessly crave-worthy oatmeal is both delicious and economic. The secret lies in the simple approach – non-dairy milk, spices, and flavorful dried fruits.

Servings 4

Ready in about 10 minutes

NUTRITIONAL INFORMATION
(Per Serving)

320 - Calories
12.6g - Fat
44.4g - Carbs
10.5g - Protein
17.2g - Sugars

Ingredients

- 1/3 cup golden raisins
- 2 tablespoons maple syrup
- 1/3 cup dried cherries
- 1/2 cup walnuts, chopped
- 1 ¼ cups steel-cut oats
- 1 cinnamon stick
- 1/2 teaspoon pure almond extract
- 1 vanilla paste
- 1 ½ cups soy milk
- 1 ½ cups water

Directions

1. Add the water, soy milk, steel-cut oats, cinnamon stick, vanilla paste, and almond extract to the cooker. Use "Manual" and cook for 10 minutes.
2. Then, let the pressure come down; open the pot following manufacturer's instructions.
3. Discard cinnamon sticks and stir in the remaining ingredients. Serve warm.

– VEGAN –

97. Banana and Chia Seed Porridge

Here's a great energy booster for your busy mornings. In addition, chia seeds are a good source of protein, fiber, vitamins, minerals, and omega-3 fats.

Servings 2

Ready in about 6 minutes

NUTRITIONAL INFORMATION (Per Serving)

657 - Calories
54.8g - Fat
41.3g - Carbs
12.2g - Protein
22.8g - Sugars

Ingredients

- 2 tablespoons Chia seeds
- 1/2 cup green apple, grated
- 1/2 cup macadamia nuts, ground
- 1/2 cup fresh mixed berries
- 1 ¼ cups coconut milk
- 1/2 teaspoon cinnamon
- 1/2 teaspoon ground cloves
- 1 cup ripe bananas

Directions

1. Add all of the above ingredients, except for the fresh berries, to your cooker.
2. Set the machine to cook for 6 minutes at HIGH pressure. Then, use the quick-release method.
3. Serve in individual dishes topped with fresh mixed berries.

– VEGAN –

98. Wheat Berry Salad with Cranberries

This easy salad is surprisingly delicious. Just toss cooked wheat berries in a salad bowl with some veggies, spices and nuts, and you're good to go!

Servings 6

Ready in about 25 minutes + chilling time

NUTRITIONAL INFORMATION (Per Serving)

157 - Calories
7.6g - Fat
19.5g - Carbs
3.6g - Protein
0.8g - Sugars

Ingredients

- 2 tablespoons extra-virgin olive oil
- 3 cups water
- 1 ½ cups wheat berries
- 3/4 cup dried cranberries
- 1 teaspoon white pepper
- 1 teaspoon sea salt
- 2 medium-sized shallots, chopped
- 1 ½ teaspoons yellow mustard
- 1/2 cup apple cider vinegar
- 1/3 cup hazelnuts, chopped

Directions

1. The night before, soak the wheat berries in cold water. Rinse them and drain.
2. Transfer the soaked wheat berries to the Instant Pot; add 3 cups of water. Now, pressure cook for about 25 minutes. Drain and transfer to a salad bowl. Add the rest of the above ingredients.
3. Lastly, refrigerate the salad overnight or at least 2 hours. Enjoy!

– VEGAN –

99. Hearty Mushroom-Bean Soup

This is a healthy and protein soup where mushrooms and beans make a great blend. Serve with crisp bread crackers.

Servings 4

Ready in about 20 minutes

NUTRITIONAL INFORMATION (Per Serving)

320 - Calories
2.0g - Fat
58.9g - Carbs
22.7g - Protein
11.5g - Sugars

Ingredients

- 4 ½ cups vegetable stock, preferably homemade
- 1 ¼ cups canned white beans
- 1/4 teaspoon freshly ground black pepper
- 1/2 teaspoon sea salt
- 1 cup carrots, trimmed and thinly sliced
- 1/2 cup celery stalk, finely chopped
- 1/2 cup parsnip, chopped
- 1 teaspoon minced garlic
- 2 small-sized onions, chopped
- 1 ½ cups crushed fresh tomatoes
- 1 ½ pounds mushrooms, thinly sliced
- 1 teaspoon dried basil
- 1 teaspoon dried oregano

Directions

1. Place all the ingredients into the Instant Pot; stir until everything is well combined.
2. Cover with the lid and secure it; choose "Manual" function and HIGH pressure for 22 minutes. Serve hot.

– VEGAN –

100. Sunday Barley Congee

This simple and delicious congee is just as good with everyday dinner, as it is served on special occasion as a side dish.

Servings 2

Ready in about 30 minutes

NUTRITIONAL INFORMATION
(Per Serving)

376 - Calories
0.9g - Fat
84.8g - Carbs
8.1g - Protein
0.9g - Sugars

Ingredients

- 1 pound purple yam, cubed
- 1/2 cup pot barley
- 1/4 cup buckwheat
- 1/4 cup rice
- 1/2 teaspoon kosher salt, or more to taste
- 1/2 teaspoon allspice

Directions

1. Add all of the above ingredients to the Instant Pot. Pour in about 8 cups of water.
2. Close the cooker's lid. Select the "Porridge" button and cook for 30 minutes.
3. Sweeten with agave syrup if desired. Serve warm.

– VEGAN –

101. Prune and Pear Vegan Oatmeal

Vegan oatmeal is a must-have for breakfast! Oats are whole-grain cereals that are high in fiber, antioxidants, vitamins, minerals. Prunes protect against chronic illnesses, reduce the risk of osteoporosis and improve circulation. Bon appétit!

Servings 2

Ready in about 20 minutes

NUTRITIONAL INFORMATION
(Per Serving)

359 - Calories
5.0g - Fat
72.9g - Carbs
10.4g - Protein
32.3g - Sugars

Ingredients

- 3/4 cup steel-cut oats
- 1 ¼ cups soy milk
- 1/2 teaspoon vanilla paste
- A pinch of cinnamon powder
- 1 ½ cups water
- 1 pear, chopped
- 6 prunes, pitted and halved

Directions

1. Put all of the above ingredients into the inner pot.
2. Select "Manual" mode; cook for 10 minutes.
3. Use the natural pressure release method. Serve warm and enjoy.

– VEGAN –

102. Bean and Apple Salad

With this easy-to-follow recipe, you can turn an ordinary vegan salad into something spectacular! This surprisingly delicious combo may become a family favorite.

Servings 8

Ready in about 35 minutes

NUTRITIONAL INFORMATION
(Per Serving)

251 - Calories
0.7g - Fat
50.2g - Carbs
13.2g - Protein
13.5g - Sugars

Ingredients

- 1 cup onions, chopped fine
- 4 cloves garlic, finely minced
- 1/4 teaspoon black pepper, or more to taste
- 1/2 teaspoon red pepper flakes, crushed
- 1/2 tablespoon dry oregano
- 1/2 tablespoon fresh basil
- 1/2 teaspoon sea salt
- 1/3 cup brown sugar
- 16 ounces red kidney beans
- 2 crisp apples, cored and diced

Directions

1. Soak the kidney beans overnight.
2. Then, transfer the soaked beans to the inner pot along with the remaining ingredients. Add water (2 inches above the top of beans).
3. Cook for 35 minutes. Serve well-chilled.

– VEGAN –

103. Sweet Potato Soup with Peanut Butter

There are a lot of recipes for sweet potato soup. But, this recipe may become your favorite because it is silky and creamy, and turns out great each and every time!

Servings 6

Ready in about 10 minutes

NUTRITIONAL INFORMATION (Per Serving)

352 - Calories
25.7g - Fat
28.1g - Carbs
6.9g - Protein
5.2g - Sugars

Ingredients

- 4 sweet potatoes, cubed
- 12 ounces canned coconut milk
- 1/2 tablespoon lemon juice
- 2 ¼ cups vegetable stock
- 1 cup tomatoes, seeded and chopped
- 3 cloves garlic, finely chopped
- 1 ¼ cups scallions, chopped
- 1/3 cup peanut butter
- 2 tablespoons grapeseed oil
- 1/2 teaspoon black pepper, to taste
- 1/2 teaspoon sea salt
- A pinch of allspice

Directions

1. Choose the "Sauté" function. Then, heat the oil, and sauté the scallions and garlic, stirring frequently, until they are softened (about 5 minutes). Press the "Cancel" button.
2. Stir in the other ingredients; stir until everything is combined well.
3. Close the lid and choose "Manual". Let it cook for about 5 minutes. Remove the lid according to the manufacturer's instructions.
4. Puree the soup to your desired consistency with an immersion blender. Serve warm.

– VEGAN –

104. Creamed Summer Squash Soup

Yellow summer squash is also known as Straightneck squash. For the best results with this soup, use a firm and small plant with bright yellow skin.

Servings 8

Ready in about 20 minutes

NUTRITIONAL INFORMATION (Per Serving)

107 - Calories
1.9g - Fat
17.8g - Carbs
6.8g - Protein
5.6g - Sugars

Ingredients

- 2 cups vegetable stock
- 2 potatoes, diced
- 14 ounces silken tofu, pressed
- 1 ½ cups boiling water
- 1 cup bell peppers, diced
- 1 cup onions, peeled and chopped
- 2 zucchinis, shredded
- 1/2 teaspoon cumin powder
- 1/2 teaspoon paprika
- 2 pounds yellow summer squash, shredded

Directions

1. Choose the "Sauté" mode; then, sauté the onions until tender and translucent or about 5 minutes.
2. Add the remaining ingredients and choose the "Soup" mode; cook for 15 minutes.
3. Remove the lid according to the manufacturer's directions. Allow it to cool before blending with an immersion blender.
4. Serve topped with fresh chopped parsley. Enjoy!

– VEGAN –

105. Easiest and Tastiest Hummus Ever

Hummus is a great addition to any vegan menu, it is simply irreplaceable if you plan to wow your vegan friends. You can substitute a lime juice for freshly squeezed lemon juice.

Servings 12

Ready in about 25 minutes

NUTRITIONAL INFORMATION
(Per Serving)

166 - Calories
9.9g - Fat
15.8g - Carbs
4.9g - Protein
2.8g - Sugars

Ingredients

- 1/2 cup extra-virgin olive oil
- 5 cups water
- 1/2 tablespoon salt
- 1/4 cup fresh lime juice
- 1 ½ cups chickpeas
- 4 garlic cloves, minced

Directions

1. Add the chickpeas and water to your cooker and drizzle with some olive oil.
2. Secure the lid and cook for 22 minutes. Turn it off and let it release the pressure. Open the lid and drain chickpeas.
3. Transfer them to a food processor, along with lime juice, garlic and salt; blitz the mixture into a smooth puree.
4. While the food processor is still running, gradually add olive oil. Serve and enjoy!

– VEGAN –

106. Homemade Mushroom Pâté

If you love mushrooms, the pressure cooker is a great tool to prepare this all-in-one spread while saving you time and money. You can add the other combo of seasonings.

Servings 16

Ready in about 17 minutes

NUTRITIONAL INFORMATION
(Per Serving)

49 - Calories
3.1g - Fat
3.4g - Carbs
2.4g - Protein
1.6g - Sugars

Ingredients

- 1/3 cup dry white wine
- 1 teaspoon dill weed
- 1/2 teaspoon marjoram
- 1/4 teaspoon black pepper, freshly cracked
- 2 sprigs thyme
- 1/2 teaspoon salt
- 2 ½ pounds fresh mushrooms, thinly sliced
- 3 cloves garlic, crushed
- 1 cup onions, peeled and sliced
- 1/4 cup butter

Directions

1. Press the "Sauté" button. When the cooker is hot, warm the butter. Now, sauté the onion and garlic until they're softened, about 5 minutes. Then, stir in the mushrooms; continue to sauté until they're fragrant and lightly browned.
2. Pour in the white wine and allow it to evaporate completely. Season with spices and herbs.
3. Close and lock the cooker's lid. Press "Manual" and choose 11-minute pressure cooking time.
4. To make the pâté: puree the ingredients using an immersion blender. Serve chilled over toast.

– VEGAN –

107. Baby Carrots with Goat Cheese and Almonds

Baby carrots are not only a lunch box staple; they have become a very popular snack in recent years. Baby carrots go perfectly with almonds and goat cheese in this refreshing appetizer recipe.

Servings 8

Ready in about 30 minutes

NUTRITIONAL INFORMATION
(Per Serving)

193 - Calories
12.3g - Fat
14.9g - Carbs
6.7g - Protein
9.4g - Sugars

Ingredients

- 1 ½ tablespoons fresh orange juice
- 3 cups water
- 2 ½ tablespoons ghee, melted
- 1 ½ cups goat cheese
- 3 tablespoons almonds, roughly chopped
- 1 tablespoon honey
- 1 teaspoon kosher salt, to taste
- 2 ½ pounds baby carrots
- 2 ½ tablespoons apple cider vinegar

Directions

1. Add the baby carrots and water to the inner pot. Close the lid and select "Manual" setting; cook for 10 minutes.
2. Drain and rinse the carrots. Transfer them to a serving dish.
3. To make the vinaigrette, combine the vinegar, orange juice, honey, kosher salt, and melted ghee.
4. Drizzle the vinaigrette over prepared baby carrots. Let it cool for 20 minutes. Serve garnished with goat cheese and almonds. Enjoy!

– VEGAN –

108. Spiced Acorn Squash Appetizer

This appetizer can be made ahead. Thus, you may need to add some non-dairy milk to thin it down before serving.

Servings 6

Ready in about 15 minutes

NUTRITIONAL INFORMATION (Per Serving)

105 - Calories
5.0g - Fat
16.3g - Carbs
1.3g - Protein
0.5g - Sugars

Ingredients

- 1 cup water
- 2 ½ tablespoons butter
- 1/3 teaspoon baking soda
- 1/4 teaspoon freshly grated nutmeg
- 2 pounds acorn squash, stem trimmed, halved and seeded
- 1/2 teaspoon salt
- 1 teaspoon brown sugar

Directions

1. Pressure cook the acorn squash. Sprinkle the cut side of the acorn squash with the salt and the baking soda.
2. Put a cooking rack into the Instant Pot. Pour in the water and lay the squash on top. Lock the lid; bring the cooker up to HIGH pressure.
3. Lower the heat to maintain high pressure and cook for 15 minutes. Quick release the pressure. Now let the squash cool.
4. Mash the squash using a potato masher. Add the butter, brown sugar, and nutmeg. Taste and adjust the seasonings.

– VEGAN –

109. Warm Russet Potato Appetizer

If you want to save some extra time in this recipe, use a store-bought vegetable stock or a vegetable bouillon cubes.

Servings 6

Ready in about 14 minutes

NUTRITIONAL INFORMATION (Per Serving)

177 - Calories
8.0g - Fat
24.5g - Carbs
2.9g - Protein
1.9g - Sugars

Ingredients

- 3/4 cup vegetable stock
- 1 teaspoon sea salt
- 1 teaspoon cayenne pepper
- 1/2 teaspoon ground black pepper, to your liking
- 1 teaspoon dried rosemary
- 2 pounds russet potatoes, cut into wedges
- 1/2 teaspoon cumin powder
- 1/2 teaspoon garlic powder
- 1/2 stick butter, softened

Directions

1. Press the "Sauté" button and add the butter; heat until it is warmed through. Now, add the potatoes and cook for about 7 minutes.
2. Add the rest of the ingredients. Secure the lid according to manufacturer's directions; press the "Manual" button. Cook for 9 minutes. Transfer to a serving platter and serve.

– VEGAN –

110. Steamed Lemony Artichokes

Feel free to use fresh orange juice instead of lemon juice as well as another combo of seasonings; dried rosemary, marjoram, and ground cumin work well! You can easily double or triple this recipe, too.

Servings 2

Ready in about 30 minutes

NUTRITIONAL INFORMATION
(Per Serving)

157 - Calories
0.6g - Fat
34.6g - Carbs
10.8g - Protein
3.5g - Sugars

Ingredients

- 1 ¼ cups water
- 1 teaspoon cayenne pepper, to taste
- 4 small-sized artichokes
- 1 teaspoon dried dill weed
- 2 tablespoons fresh lemon juice

Directions

1. Rinse the artichokes; remove any outer leaves. Now, trim off the stem and the top third of each artichoke with a sharp knife. Drizzle with the lemon juice. Sprinkle with dill weed and cayenne pepper.
2. Set a steamer basket into your Instant Pot. Pour the water into the base of your cooker. Stack the artichokes in the steamer basket; pour in 1½ cups of water.
3. Choose "Manual" mode; adjust the time to 22 minutes. Serve with the sauce of choice.

– VEGAN –

111. Orange-Glazed Chicken Wings

Here's a stress-free recipe for your party dinner! A big bowl of sticky chicken wings is a real crowd-pleaser.

Servings 6

Ready in about 13 minutes

NUTRITIONAL INFORMATION
(Per Serving)

322 - Calories
9.3g - Fat
13.7g - Carbs
44.1g - Protein
11.5g - Sugars

Ingredients

- 1 cup medium green onions, thinly sliced
- 12 boneless, skinless chicken thighs, trimmed
- 2 tablespoons olive oil
- 1/3 cup orange marmalade
- 1/4 teaspoon ground black pepper
- 1/2 teaspoon salt
- 3 tablespoons balsamic vinegar

Directions

1. Use a fork to whisk the marmalade and balsamic vinegar in a small mixing bowl; reserve.
2. Heat the olive oil in your Instant Pot turned to the "Sauté" function. Season the chicken with salt and ground black pepper. Transfer the mixture to the Instant Pot.
3. Pour the marmalade-vinegar mixture over the chicken. Lock the lid onto the cooker. Cook for 13 minutes at HIGH pressure.
4. Use the quick-release method to bring the pot's pressure back to normal. Sprinkle with green onions and serve warm.

– VEGAN –

112. Rich Sausage and Tomato Dip

Your family and guests are going to have a hard time resisting this rich, chunky, and flavorful dipping sauce. This dipping sauce pairs well with tortilla chips, carrot sticks, and garlic saltines.

Servings 10

Ready in about 30 minutes

NUTRITIONAL INFORMATION
(Per Serving)

233 - Calories
15.7g - Fat
11.5g - Carbs
11.5g - Protein
4.8g - Sugars

Ingredients

- 3 cloves garlic, sliced
- 1 cup shallots, finely chopped
- 1 teaspoon dried rosemary
- 1/2 teaspoon dried basil
- 1 teaspoon dried oregano
- 2 ½ tablespoons flour
- 2 tablespoons olive oil
- 30 ounces canned crushed tomatoes
- 1/2 teaspoon ground black pepper, or more to taste
- 1 teaspoon salt
- 1 pound ground sausage meat

Directions

1. Heat the olive oil in the cooker. Stir in the sausage meat and cook for 7 minutes, or until it's browned. Add the other ingredients.
2. Close and lock the lid according to the manufacturer's directions; set the timer for 18 minutes.
3. Afterwards, release the pressure naturally. Serve with corn tortilla chips.

– VEGAN –

113. Appetizer Meatballs in Tomato Sauce

Looking for a quick and easy recipe for a holiday cocktail party? What could be better than small meatballs dipped in ambrosial tomato sauce? Yummy!

Servings 10

Ready in about 30 minutes

NUTRITIONAL INFORMATION
(Per Serving)

224 - Calories
14.5g - Fat
11.9g - Carbs
19.1g - Protein
4.9g - Sugars

Ingredients

- 3/4 cup vegetable stock
- 1/2 teaspoon ground black pepper, or more to taste
- 1 teaspoon sea salt
- 30 ounces tomato sauce
- 2 tablespoons olive oil
- 38 frozen meatballs
- 1/3 cup fresh parsley, chopped

Directions

1. Warm the olive oil in the cooker on "Sauté" setting. Stir in the meatballs and cook until they are browned. Cook for 3 minutes; gently stir to combine.
2. Add the tomato sauce and vegetable stock. Sprinkle with salt, black pepper, and parsley. Close and lock the lid according to the manufacturer's directions.
3. Set the timer for 22 minutes. Release the pressure naturally. Serve warm.

– VEGAN –

114. Classic Buffalo Chicken Wings

These chicken wings are so addictive, so you might want to make an extra batch! In addition, you don't need to have any special culinary skills to make this classic. Win-win!

Servings 4

Ready in about 20 minutes

NUTRITIONAL INFORMATION (Per Serving)

371 - Calories
7.3g - Fat
70.1g - Carbs
10.9g - Protein
2.2g - Sugars

Ingredients

- 5 teaspoons sesame oil
- 3 cloves garlic, smashed
- 1 medium-sized leek, peeled and sliced
- 7 cups water
- 2 ¼ cups white wheat berries, soaked overnight
- 5 medium-sized potatoes, cubed
- 1/4 teaspoon ground black pepper, or more to taste
- 1 teaspoon seasoned salt
- 1 teaspoon dried thyme

Directions

1. Combine the white wheat berries with water in your Instant Pot.
2. In a medium-sized skillet, warm the sesame oil over medium-high flame. Then, sauté the leeks and garlic until tender. Stir in the thyme; cook for 1 more minute, stirring a few times.
3. Choose "Multi-grain" function; cook your wheat together with potatoes for about 20 minutes.
4. When the mixture is ready, add sautéed leeks with garlic.
5. Sprinkle with seasoned salt and black pepper to taste. Serve.

– VEGAN –

115. Tomato Pork Dip

This chunky and flavorful dip may become your holiday-favorite! Serve with breadsticks or potato chips.

Servings 4

Ready in about 20 minutes

NUTRITIONAL INFORMATION
(Per Serving)

371 - Calories
7.3g - Fat
70.1g - Carbs
10.9g - Protein
2.2g - Sugars

Ingredients

- 5 teaspoons sesame oil
- 3 cloves garlic, smashed
- 1 medium-sized leek, peeled and sliced
- 7 cups water
- 2 ¼ cups white wheat berries, soaked overnight
- 5 medium-sized potatoes, cubed
- 1/4 teaspoon ground black pepper, or more to taste
- 1 teaspoon seasoned salt
- 1 teaspoon dried thyme

Directions

1. Combine the white wheat berries with water in your Instant Pot.
2. In a medium-sized skillet, warm the sesame oil over medium-high flame. Then, sauté the leeks and garlic until tender. Stir in the thyme; cook for 1 more minute, stirring a few times.
3. Choose "Multi-grain" function; cook your wheat together with potatoes for about 20 minutes.
4. When the mixture is ready, add sautéed leeks with garlic.
5. Sprinkle with seasoned salt and black pepper to taste. Serve.

– VEGAN –

116. Kale and Carrot Appetizer

Kale is a good source of valuable antioxidants, vitamin C, vitamin K, beta-carotene, minerals and so forth. Carrots are loaded with beta-carotene, vitamin B6, and vitamin K.

Servings 4

Ready in about 20 minutes

NUTRITIONAL INFORMATION
(Per Serving)

371 - Calories
7.3g - Fat
70.1g - Carbs
10.9g - Protein
2.2g - Sugars

Ingredients

- 5 teaspoons sesame oil
- 3 cloves garlic, smashed
- 1 medium-sized leek, peeled and sliced
- 7 cups water
- 2 ¼ cups white wheat berries, soaked overnight
- 5 medium-sized potatoes, cubed
- 1/4 teaspoon ground black pepper, or more to taste
- 1 teaspoon seasoned salt
- 1 teaspoon dried thyme

Directions

1. Combine the white wheat berries with water in your Instant Pot.
2. In a medium-sized skillet, warm the sesame oil over medium-high flame. Then, sauté the leeks and garlic until tender. Stir in the thyme; cook for 1 more minute, stirring a few times.
3. Choose "Multi-grain" function; cook your wheat together with potatoes for about 20 minutes.
4. When the mixture is ready, add sautéed leeks with garlic.
5. Sprinkle with seasoned salt and black pepper to taste. Serve.

– VEGAN –

117. Cheesy Corn Dip

You can make this dipping sauce up to two days in advance! It is great dish for your party or a snack to bridge the breakfast-lunch gap. Enjoy!

Servings 12

Ready in about 20 minutes

NUTRITIONAL INFORMATION (Per Serving)

288 - Calories
25.1g - Fat
12.9g - Carbs
5.0g - Protein
2.6g - Sugars

Ingredients

- 2 cups green onions, chopped
- 1/2 teaspoon dried dill weed
- 1/4 teaspoon white pepper to taste
- 1 teaspoon paprika
- 1 teaspoon salt
- 1 cup mayonnaise
- 1 ¼ cups sour cream
- 2 pounds corn kernels, frozen
- 16 ounces sharp cheese, shredded

Directions

1. Add corn kernels to your Instant Pot. Choose the "Steam" setting and adjust the timer for 5 minutes. Transfer to a large-sized bowl and allow it to cool for 15 minutes.
2. Add the remaining ingredients; stir to combine well. Cover the bowl and refrigerate your dip until it is ready to serve.

– VEGAN –

118. Potato Mash with Marjoram

Healthy snacking is the best way to maintain the ideal body weight, stay healthy and fuel your energy level through the day. Actually, potatoes provide valuable energy-delivering complex carbohydrates as well as vitamins and minerals.

Servings 4

Ready in about 20 minutes

NUTRITIONAL INFORMATION
(Per Serving)

60 - Calories
1.1g - Fat
11.6g - Carbs
2.5g - Protein
1.7g - Sugars

Ingredients

- 4 cloves garlic, sliced
- 1 ¼ cups vegetable stock
- 1/2 teaspoon ground black pepper
- 1 teaspoon sea salt
- 1 teaspoon mustard powder
- 1/2 teaspoon onion powder
- 1 pound Yukon Gold potatoes, diced
- 1/3 cup non-dairy milk
- 1/4 cup fresh marjoram, for garnish

Directions

1. Place the potatoes, vegetable stock, and garlic in your Instant Pot.
2. Close the lid and select "Manual" function; adjust the time to 10 minutes.
3. Carefully open the cooker. Mash the potatoes, adding the non-dairy milk, onion powder, mustard powder, salt, and black pepper.
4. Serve immediately garnished with fresh marjoram. Enjoy!

– VEGAN –

119. Herby Polenta Squares with Cheese

Snack smarter with this Italian classic! The electric pressure cooker keeps the polenta plump and moist, a good match for the cheese and fresh herbs.

Servings 6

Ready in about 35 minutes

NUTRITIONAL INFORMATION (Per Serving)

235 - Calories
7.6g - Fat
33.1g - Carbs
8.2g - Protein
4.5g - Sugars

Ingredients

- 1 ¼ cups dry polenta
- 1/2 teaspoon cayenne pepper
- 1 teaspoon salt
- 2 ½ cups soy milk
- 1 ½ cups water
- 2 tablespoons butter, room temperature
- 1/2 cup Ricotta cheese, for garnish
- 1 tablespoon fresh marjoram, for garnish
- 1 tablespoon fresh chopped Italian parsley, for garnish

Directions

1. Simply fill your Instant Pot with the water, soy milk, butter, salt, and cayenne pepper. Press the "Sauté" key.
2. Gradually stir the polenta into the boiling liquid, stirring continuously. Cover, push the "Manual" button and set the timer for 6 minutes.
3. Next, release the pressure naturally. Pour the polenta mixture into a baking sheet. Refrigerate it for 25 minutes. Cut into squares and transfer to a plate.
4. Sprinkle with fresh parsley and marjoram; serve topped with ricotta cheese.

– VEGAN –

120. Delicious Fingerling Potatoes

If you've never had fingerling potatoes from the Instant Pot, you're missing the most flavorful potatoes ever! You can substitute rosemary for thyme or cilantro if desired.

Servings 6

Ready in about 20 minutes

NUTRITIONAL INFORMATION
(Per Serving)

200 - Calories
7.5g - Fat
30.8g - Carbs
4.3g - Protein
2.0g - Sugars

Ingredients
- 3/4 cup vegetable broth
- 2 ½ pounds fingerling potatoes
- 1 teaspoon dried dill weed
- 1 teaspoon sea salt
- 1/2 teaspoon cayenne pepper
- 1/2 teaspoon ground black pepper, or more to your liking
- 2 sprigs rosemary
- 3 garlic cloves, with outer skin
- 3 tablespoons olive oil

Directions
1. Use the "Sauté" function to preheat your Instant Pot. Warm the olive oil; when the oil is hot, stir in the fingerling potatoes, rosemary, dill weed, and garlic; cook for 6 minutes.
2. Cook the fingerling potatoes, turning once or twice, for about 11 minutes. Now, pierce in the middle of each potato with a sharp knife. Stir in the vegetable broth, salt, ground black pepper, cayenne pepper to your liking.
3. Choose the "Manual" function and cook for 6 minutes. Afterward, use a quick pressure release. Allow the garlic cloves to cool; peel and smash them.
4. Taste, adjust the seasonings and serve.

– VEGAN –

121. Squash and Pineapple Treat

There's nothing like a light and easy summer meal that is loaded with valuable nutrients. Summer squash is high in Vitamin A, C and B6, fiber, riboflavin, magnesium, potassium, and phosphorus.

Servings 8

Ready in about 20 minutes

NUTRITIONAL INFORMATION
(Per Serving)

200 - Calories
7.5g - Fat
30.8g - Carbs
4.3g - Protein
2.0g - Sugars

Ingredients

- 3 summer squashes, cut into bite-sized pieces
- 2 teaspoons brown sugar
- 2 tablespoons arrowroot combined with 3 tablespoons water
- 1 cup shallots, diced
- 1/4 teaspoon freshly ground black pepper, or more to your liking
- 1/2 teaspoon sea salt
- 2 ½ tablespoons soy sauce
- 1/3 cup pineapple juice
- 2 tablespoons olive oil
- 10 ounces canned pineapple chunks

Directions

1. Select the "Sauté" function; warm the olive oil; now, sauté the shallot for about 5 minutes. Add the squash, pineapple chunks, pineapple juice, and soy sauce; stir to combine well.
2. Next, lock the lid. Choose the "Manual" function and cook for 12 minutes. Quick release the pressure.
3. Combine the rest of the ingredients in a small-sized mixing bowl. Add the mixture to the pot to thicken the liquid. Serve.

122. Cremini Mushrooms and Asparagus Appetizer

Here's a skinny recipe to try right now! Very low in saturated fat and high in minerals and dietary fiber, this recipe is sure to please.

Servings 6

Ready in about 10 minutes

NUTRITIONAL INFORMATION
(Per Serving)

42 - Calories
0.4g - Fat
8.2g - Carbs
3.9g - Protein
3.8g - Sugars

Ingredients

- 3 tablespoons water
- 2 cups scallions, thinly sliced
- 1/2 teaspoon ground black pepper
- 1 teaspoon sea salt
- 1/2 teaspoon garlic powder
- 1/2 teaspoon cumin powder
- 2 cups asparagus, chopped
- 3 cups sliced cremini mushrooms

Directions

1. Click the "Sauté" key and cook the mushrooms and scallions until tender, for about 2 minutes.
2. Add the rest of the ingredients. Lock the lid and cook on HIGH pressure; set the timer for 3 minutes. Quick release the pressure.
3. Transfer to a large serving platter and serve.

– VEGAN –

123. Chili Pumpkin Hummus

If you haven't cooked hummus in the Instant pot before, it can be a little challenging to make this recipe. If you tend to use canned chickpeas, just drop them into your pot. However, if you tend to use raw chickpeas, allow them to soak overnight. Pre-soaking will shorten the cooking time and make your chickpeas more digestible.

Servings 16

Ready in about 35 minutes

NUTRITIONAL INFORMATION
(Per Serving)

172 - Calories
7.6g - Fat
21.5g - Carbs
6.4g - Protein
3.5g - Sugars

Ingredients

- 6 cups water
- 1 ½ cups canned pumpkin puree
- 1/3 cup olive oil
- 2 ½ tablespoons tahini
- 2 tablespoons soy sauce
- 1/2 tablespoon cilantro paste
- 4 garlic cloves, minced
- 2 cups shallots, peeled and finely minced
- 1/2 teaspoon lemon zest
- 1 ½ tablespoons lemon juice
- 2 cups chickpeas
- 2 tablespoons toasted pumpkin seeds, for garnish
- 1/4 teaspoon ground cardamom
- 2 teaspoons Dukkah spice blend
- 1 teaspoon chipotle chili powder
- 1 teaspoon crushed sea salt

Directions

1. Select the "Manual" function and cook the chickpeas in water for 23 minutes. Carefully open the cooker and drain the cooked chickpeas; transfer chickpeas to your food processor.
2. Stir in the shallot, garlic, pumpkin puree, Dukkah spice blend, and sea salt. Mix to combine.

– VEGAN –

124. Maple Brussels Sprouts

These sticky bites may become your next holiday-favorite! In addition, this snack is a good idea if you want to stay healthy and fit.

Servings 4

Ready in about 6 minutes

NUTRITIONAL INFORMATION
(Per Serving)

171 - Calories
4.3g - Fat
31.1g - Carbs
8.4g - Protein
11.7g - Sugars

Ingredients

- 20 small-sized Brussels sprouts, cut in half
- 1 ½ tablespoons maple syrup
- 1/3 cup water
- 2 medium-sized onions, diced
- 1 tablespoon sesame oil
- 1/2 teaspoon freshly ground black pepper
- 1/2 teaspoon sea salt
- 1/2 teaspoon cayenne pepper

Directions

1. Firstly, set your Instant Pot to "Sauté"; now, warm the sesame oil; sauté the onions for 3 minutes.
2. In a mixing bowl, whisk the water and maple syrup; add your Brussels sprouts to the cooker. Drizzle the maple mixture over them and sprinkle with cayenne pepper, salt, and black pepper.
3. Lock the lid and bring to HIGH pressure for 3 minutes. Quick release the pressure. Serve immediately.

– VEGAN –

125. Famous Lemon-Garlic Corn on the Cob

Seriously, how can you go wrong with corn on the cob for a snack? Corn is an appetite-suppressing food and a great solution for minimizing your hunger between meals.

Servings 6

Ready in about 10 minutes

NUTRITIONAL
INFORMATION
(Per Serving)

222 - Calories
7.2g - Fat
39.4g - Carbs
6.9g - Protein
6.8g - Sugars

Ingredients

- 3 cloves garlic, minced
- 1/2 teaspoon ground black pepper
- 1 teaspoon salt
- 8 ears of corn, shucked
- 1 ½ tablespoons lemon juice
- 2 ½ tablespoons butter, room temperature
- 1 tablespoon basil leaves, chopped

Directions

1. Firstly, place the ears of corn on the metal rack in your cooker. Make sure to add 1 cup of water and seal the lid.
2. Select the "Manual" setting; adjust the cooking time to 5 minutes. Carefully open the lid by following the manufacturer's instructions.
3. Meanwhile, heat up a pan over medium heat. Now, melt the butter and sauté the garlic along with the dried basil for 5 minutes or until they are fragrant. Let it cool slightly; then, add the lemon juice, salt, and black pepper.
4. Transfer the prepared ears of corn to a serving. Drizzle the pan sauce over ears of corn and serve.

BEANS & GRAINS

– Beans & Grains –

126. Yummy Apple Oatmeal

When you're looking for just the right thing to serve for your family breakfast, this fruity oatmeal will fit the bill. You might need to make a double batch because it disappears almost as fast as you can make it!

Servings 4

Ready in about 25 minutes

NUTRITIONAL INFORMATION (Per Serving)

239 - Calories
5.4g - Fat
46.7g - Carbs
4.6g - Protein
29.5g - Sugars

Ingredients

- 2 ½ cups water
- 1/3 cup honey
- 1/3 cup sliced almonds
- 1 cup dried apples, chopped
- 1 cup steel-cut oats
- 1/2 teaspoon ground cinnamon
- 1/2 teaspoon salt

Directions

1. Mix everything in your Instant Pot. Lock the cooker's.
2. Set the machine to cook at HIGH pressure. Set the timer to cook for 19 minutes.
3. Turn off the machine. Allow the pot's pressure to return to normal.
4. Unlock and open your Instant Pot; stir well and serve.

— BEANS & GRAINS —

127. Raisin-Cinnamon Rice Pudding

Warm, creamy, and delicious, this rice pudding is a true comfort in a bowl! You can substitute golden raisins for dried cranberries and basmati rice for white rice; cooking time remains the same.

Servings 6

Ready in about 30 minutes

NUTRITIONAL INFORMATION (Per Serving)

580 - Calories
16.4g - Fat
92.1g - Carbs
17.1g - Protein
23.9g - Sugars

Ingredients

- 3 whole eggs
- 3/4 cup golden raisins
- 1 teaspoon kosher salt
- 1 ¼ cups half-and-half
- 2 cups basmati rice
- 1/3 cup agave nectar
- 1 teaspoon ground cinnamon
- 6 cups whole milk

Directions

1. In the inner pot, combine the basmati rice, agave nectar, kosher salt, and milk. Choose the "Sauté" function; bring to a boil and cook for 5 minutes. Give it a good stir.
2. Cover the instant pot. Press the "Rice" button and 17-minute cook time; perform the quick pressure release
3. Meanwhile, whisk the eggs and half-and-half until well combined.
4. Remove the lid from the pot. Add the egg mixture, golden raisins, and cinnamon. Press the "Sauté" button.
5. Continue cooking until it starts to boil. Turn off the pot. Serve immediately.

– BEANS & GRAINS –

128. Date Cinnamon Bread Pudding

This aromatic bread pudding is a great way to start your morning. It is also delicious and very satisfying with eggs and whole milk.

Servings 4

Ready in about 45 minutes

NUTRITIONAL INFORMATION
(Per Serving)

319 - Calories
10.5g - Fat
47.4g - Carbs
12.5g - Protein
45.7g - Sugars

Ingredients

- Nonstick cooking spray
- 1/4 teaspoon salt
- 1/2 cup dried dates, pitted and chopped
- 1/3 cup honey
- 1/4 teaspoon cinnamon powder
- 2 ½ cups whole milk
- 2 whole eggs plus 3 egg yolks
- 8 slices cinnamon bread, torn into pieces
- 1/4 teaspoon ground cloves
- 1 teaspoon vanilla paste

Directions

1. Treat a 6-cup bowl with a butter-flavored nonstick cooking spray. Drop cinnamon bread pieces into the bowl.
2. In a separate bowl, mix the rest of the components, except for the dates. Pour this custard mixture over the bread pieces. Scatter chopped dates over the top. Let stand for about 22 minutes. Cover the bowl tightly with a piece of greased foil.
3. Put a rack into the inner pot; pour in 2½ cups of water.
4. Lock the cooker's lid. Use "Manual" setting on HIGH and cook for 20 minutes. Afterwards, use a natural release method.

– BEANS & GRAINS –

129. Nutty Bulgur and Oat Porridge

Bulgur is a versatile food and you can make it at a moment's notice! This time, we choose the combination with oats and walnuts but you can come up with your own combo of ingredients.

Servings 8

Ready in about 30 minutes

NUTRITIONAL INFORMATION
(Per Serving)

175 - Calories
4.0g - Fat
32.6g - Carbs
4.8g - Protein
11.8g - Sugars

Ingredients

- 1/3 cup honey
- 1 cup steel-cut oats
- 1 cup bulgur
- 1/2 teaspoon ground cloves
- 1/2 teaspoon ground cinnamon
- 1/4 teaspoon freshly grated nutmeg
- 1/3 cup walnuts, chopped
- 4 ½ cups water

Directions

1. Mix everything in your Instant Pot. Lock the lid onto the Instant Pot. Set the machine to cook at HIGH pressure. Cook for 27 minutes.
2. Use the quick-release method and remove the lid. Set the cooker to its "Sauté" function. Bring to a simmer; cook for 3 more minutes.

– BEANS & GRAINS –

130. Cheese and Tabasco Grits

These cheesy and buttery grits are a great way to start your morning; it can be healthy and satisfying dinner as well. Monterey Jack cheese works well, too.

Ingredients

- 1 ¼ cups Colby cheese, grated
- 3 tablespoons butter
- 3 cups water
- 1 ½ cups corn grits
- 1/2 teaspoon salt
- A few drizzles of Tabasco sauce, to taste

Servings 6

Ready in about 25 minutes

NUTRITIONAL INFORMATION
(Per Serving)

173 - Calories
13.7g - Fat
6.5g - Carbs
6.3g - Protein
0.9g - Sugars

Directions

1. Pour 2 cups of water into a cooking pot. Make an aluminum foil sling and set a soufflé dish.
2. Mix the grits, butter, salt, and water in the baking dish. Then, lower the baking dish onto the rack in the cooker.
3. Lock the lid onto the pot. Set the machine to cook at HIGH pressure. Set the machine's timer to cook for 22 minutes.
4. Turn off the heat and remove the lid according to the manufacturer's instructions. To serve, scatter the cheese over the top and drizzle with Tabasco.

– BEANS & GRAINS –

131. Bean and Mint Salad

Whip up this salad when you want to surprise your family with something new and delicious. In this recipe, do not try to replace dry beans with canned beans.

Servings 4

Ready in about 10 minutes

NUTRITIONAL INFORMATION (Per Serving)

280 - Calories
6.0g - Fat
43.0g - Carbs
15.7g - Protein
1.5g - Sugars

Ingredients

- 4 ¼ cups water
- 1/2 teaspoon black pepper, to taste
- 1 teaspoon sea salt
- 2 bay leaves
- 2 garlic cloves, smashed
- 1 ½ tablespoons olive oil
- 1 ¼ cups dry beans, soaked
- 2 sprigs fresh mint

Directions

1. Add the soaked beans, water, garlic clove, and bay leaf to the Instant Pot.
2. Close and lock the lid. Use the "Manual" mode and choose 9-minute cooking time.
3. Use natural pressure release to open the cooker. Strain the beans and transfer to a salad bowl. Toss with the remaining ingredients. Serve chilled.

– BEANS & GRAINS –

132. Yam Barley Congee

This multigrain porridge is extra-creamy and so easy to prepare. You just need to throw all ingredients into the inner pot. To serve, you can drizzle individual portions with truffle oil or soy sauce.

Servings 12

Ready in about 50 minutes

NUTRITIONAL INFORMATION
(Per Serving)

204 - Calories
1.1g - Fat
43.4g - Carbs
5.1g - Protein
0.0g - Sugars

Ingredients

- 1 pound purple yam, cubed
- 1/2 pound barley
- 1/2 pound black eye beans
- 1/2 pound glutinous rice
- 1/2 pound brown rice
- 1/2 pound buckwheat
- 1 teaspoon salt
- 1/4 teaspoon black pepper, or more to taste

Directions

1. Add the ingredients to the inner pot. Pour in 7 cups of water.
2. Close the lid. Press the "Porridge" button and cook for 44 minutes.
3. Sweeten with honey if desired. Enjoy!

133. Butter Bean Casserole

This is a great recipe for the cooler seasons. Butter beans, also known as lima beans, are one of the most comfort foods in the world. They are high in dietary fiber and fat-free, high-quality protein.

Servings 8

Ready in about 25 minutes

NUTRITIONAL INFORMATION (Per Serving)

295 - Calories
19.8g - Fat
23.8g - Carbs
7.3g - Protein
6.0g - Sugars

Ingredients

- 1 stick butter
- 1 ¼ cups sour cream
- 2 bay leaves
- 1 teaspoon sea salt
- 3 tablespoons sugar
- 1/2 teaspoon mustard
- 1 ½ teaspoons granulated garlic
- 1 ½ pounds butter beans
- 1/2 cup fresh chopped chives, for garnish

Directions

1. Firstly, soak the butter beans with 8 cups of water. Then, add the salt and bay leaf, and press the "Manual" button. Cook for 5 minutes under HIGH pressure.
2. Press the "Keep Warm" button and leave it for 9 minutes; next, quick release pressure.
3. Drain the butter beans; add them back to the Instant Pot. Next, add the remaining ingredients, except for chives.
4. Cook for 11 minutes on "Manual" under HIGH pressure. Serve garnished with fresh chives. Enjoy!

— BEANS & GRAINS —

134. Sausage and Navy Bean Soup with Greens

If you love sausage and navy beans in the same dish, give this recipe a try. This out-of-the-box combination will amaze your family!

Servings 8

Ready in about 50 minutes

NUTRITIONAL INFORMATION
(Per Serving)

474 - Calories
28.2g - Fat
31.5g - Carbs
28.5g - Protein
4.0g - Sugars

Ingredients

- 5 cups chicken broth
- 1/4 teaspoon black pepper, to taste
- 1/2 teaspoon kosher salt
- 2 tablespoons olive oil
- 2 medium-sized onions, chopped
- 1 ½ pounds spicy sausage, sliced
- 1 ½ cups dry navy beans
- 1 teaspoon hot sauce, or more to taste
- 2 large bunches mustard greens, rinsed, stemmed and chopped

Directions

1. Place the navy beans in a large bowl and water to cover them; let them stand overnight to soak. On the next day drain and rinse the navy beans.
2. Put the soaked beans in your Instant Pot along with five cups of water. Press the "Bean/Chili" button and cook for 23 minutes. Use the natural release method to drop the pressure.
3. Bring another pot filled with salted water to a boil. Add the greens and simmer until they're wilted, approximately 3 minutes. Drain and cool under cold water. Set aside.
4. Heat the olive oil over medium heat in the pot. Brown the sausage on all sides, approximately 4 minutes. Reserve. Add the onions to the pot and cook for 4 minutes. Pour in the chicken broth.
5. Return the sausage and beans to the pot. Bring soup to a boil, reduce heat to LOW; let it simmer uncovered for 17 minutes. Add the salt, pepper, and hot sauce. Enjoy!

– BEANS & GRAINS –

135. Mushroom and Bean Vegetarian Soup

Cannellini beans work greatest for this recipe but you can freely use kidney beans or Great Northern beans. Keep in mind that your Instant pot reaches the temperature and pressure depending on the temperature of your vegetables, i.e. whether or not they are frozen.

Servings 4

Ready in about 30 minutes

NUTRITIONAL INFORMATION
(Per Serving)

400 - Calories
6.5g - Fat
64.3g - Carbs
26.4g - Protein
11.6g - Sugars

Ingredients

- 1 cup carrots, trimmed and thinly sliced
- 1 cup potatoes, diced
- 1/2 teaspoon freshly ground black pepper, to your liking
- 1 teaspoon salt
- 1 ½ cups diced zucchini
- 1/2 cup onions, chopped
- 3 cloves garlic, minced
- 3/4 pound mushrooms, chopped
- 25 ounces canned tomatoes, crushed
- 4 cups vegetable stock
- 1 ½ cups cannellini beans, cooked
- 1/2 cup Parmesan cheese, grated

Directions

1. Add all of the above ingredients to your Instant Pot; give it a good stir.
2. Seal the lid and select "Manual" mode and HIGH pressure. Cook for 22 minutes. Serve hot, topped with grated Parmesan cheese.

— BEANS & GRAINS —

136. Creamy Breakfast Risotto with Blackberries

You can whip up this delectable breakfast in just s few minutes and enjoy a lazy morning with your family! Substitute blackberries with raspberries if desired.

Servings 6

Ready in about 30 minutes

NUTRITIONAL INFORMATION
(Per Serving)

322 - Calories
4.6g - Fat
64.5g - Carbs
4.9g - Protein
10.8g - Sugars

Ingredients

- 1 ½ cups apple juice
- 2 cups Arborio rice
- 1/2 teaspoon salt
- 1 ½ cups fresh blackberries
- 1/3 cup light cream
- 3 teaspoons unsalted butter
- 1/3 teaspoon ground cinnamon
- 1 ½ tablespoons maple syrup

Directions

1. Melt the butter in your Instant Pot turned to the "Sauté" function. Stir in about 1 cup of blackberries; cook for 4 minutes, stirring often.
2. Stir in the rice, cinnamon, and salt. Cook for 2 minutes longer. Pour in the apple juice and 1¾ cups water; stir well to combine.
3. Set the machine to cook at HIGH pressure for 12 minutes. Then, use the quick-release method. Unlock and open the cooker.
4. Click the "Rice" key and add the cream and maple syrup. Simmer for about 3 minutes.
5. Unplug the machine, stir the risotto, and serve warm.

137. Polenta with Pecans and Honey

As a matter of fact, polenta is cornmeal mush that can be served in so many ways. This polenta with honey and pecans is delicious enough to have as a dessert and healthy enough to serve for breakfast without any guilt.

Servings 6

Ready in about 17 minutes

NUTRITIONAL INFORMATION
(Per Serving)

324 - Calories
13.7g - Fat
47.8g - Carbs
4.2g - Protein
16.2g - Sugars

Ingredients

- 1 cup heavy cream
- 1/3 cup honey
- 1/2 cup pecans
- 1/4 teaspoon ground white pepper
- 1/2 teaspoon salt
- 1 ½ cups polenta
- 4 ½ cups water
- 1/2 teaspoon almond extract

Directions

1. Start by adding the water to your cooker. Now, stir in the honey, pecans, and almond extract. Bring to a boil, stirring frequently. Slowly add the polenta.
2. Lock the lid onto the cooker.
3. Set the machine to cook at HIGH pressure. Then, cook for 14 minutes. Use the quick-release method to release the pressure.
4. Unlock and remove the lid. Stir in the cream; sprinkle with salt and white pepper.

— BEANS & GRAINS —

138. Chili Bean and Ham Bone Soup

When you want to please the whole family, and take all the credit for yourself, 30-minute chili soup is the right choice. This quick-fix soup is both inexpensive and satisfying.

Servings 6

Ready in about 30 minutes

NUTRITIONAL INFORMATION
(Per Serving)

187 - Calories
6.9g - Fat
17.5g - Carbs
14.7g - Protein
6.2g - Sugars

Ingredients

- 1 cup onion, chopped
- 1/2 teaspoon ground black pepper, to taste
- 1 teaspoon sea salt
- 1/2 teaspoon celery seeds
- 1 pound ham bone
- 1 bay leaf
- 20 ounces canned tomatoes, diced
- 1 ½ cups dry beans, soaked
- 1 ½ cups carrots, diced
- 1/2 teaspoon garlic powder
- 1/2 teaspoon chili powder
- 1 cup parsnip, finely chopped

Directions

1. Drain and rinse the beans. Transfer the beans along with the ham bone and bay leaves to the cooker; pour in enough water to cover them. Seal your Instant Pot and select the "Bean/Chili" mode; cook for 8 minutes.
2. Toss out the ham bone and bay leaf; add the remaining ingredients; stir to blend.
3. Choose the "Soup" setting, adjusted down to 22 minutes. Open the cooker according to manufacturer's instructions. Serve hot.

– BEANS & GRAINS –

139. Spiced Beans with Turkey

This is no ordinary beans. The addition of turkey breasts and white wine in this recipe turns an everyday taste into something spectacular!

Servings 6

Ready in about 30 minutes

NUTRITIONAL INFORMATION
(Per Serving)

242 - Calories
8.2g - Fat
19.2g - Carbs
22.6g - Protein
9.3g - Sugars

Ingredients

- 1/4 cup white wine
- 1/2 teaspoon freshly ground pepper
- 3 ½ cups chicken stock
- 1 teaspoon sea salt
- 1 ¼ pounds dried beans
- 2 medium-sized onions, diced
- 1 cup tomatoes, diced
- 3 cloves garlic, peeled and minced
- 2 ½ tablespoons vegetable oil
- 1 ½ pounds turkey breast, cut into pieces
- 2 Serrano peppers, seeded and diced
- 1 teaspoon paprika
- 1 cup bell pepper, seeded and thinly sliced
- 1 ½ tablespoons parsley

Directions

1. Press the "Sauté" button and warm the vegetable oil. Then, sear the turkey on all sides, stirring occasionally. In the pan drippings, sauté the onions, garlic, and peppers.
2. Add the remaining ingredients; add the turkey back to the cooker. Place the lid on the cooker. Press the "Bean" button and cook for 28 minutes.
3. Next, remove the lid according to the manufacturer's directions. Serve warm and enjoy!

– BEANS & GRAINS –

140. Berry Banana Rice Porridge

This tasty rice porridge can be thrown together in a snap, using convenient and inexpensive basics! Include this porridge in your weeknight menu and surprise your family!

Servings 6

Ready in about 20 minutes

NUTRITIONAL INFORMATION (Per Serving)

360 - Calories
5.2g - Fat
72.4g - Carbs
5.4g - Protein
15.2g - Sugars

Ingredients

- 1 ½ cups pineapple juice
- 2 cups basmati rice
- 1 tablespoon maple syrup
- 3 cups water
- 2 bananas, sliced
- 1/4 teaspoon grated nutmeg
- 1/4 teaspoon salt
- 1/2 teaspoon ground cloves
- 3 teaspoons butter
- 1/3 cup heavy cream
- 1 ¼ cups fresh mixed berries

Directions

1. Melt the butter in your Instant Pot turned to the "Sauté" function. Stir in the mixed berries and the slices of banana; cook for two minutes, stirring often.
2. Stir in the rice, nutmeg, cloves, and a pinch of salt. Cook for an additional minute. Pour in the water and pineapple juice; stir well to combine.
3. Set the machine to cook at HIGH pressure for 12 minutes. Then, use the quick-release method. Unlock and open the cooker.
4. Press the "Rice" button; stir in the cream and maple syrup. Simmer for about 3 minutes. Unplug the machine, stir and serve warm.

DESSERTS

– DESSERTS –

141. Fresh Currant Bread Pudding

This recipe calls for sweet bread in order to achieve a rich and delectable flavor. Banana bread, gingerbread, cardamom bread, and coffee cake or raisin bread work well. Top it with a scoop of your favorite ice cream and enjoy!

Servings 6

Ready in about 15 minutes

NUTRITIONAL INFORMATION
(Per Serving)

350 - Calories
21.6g - Fat
31.0g - Carbs
9.5g - Protein
17.1g - Sugars

Ingredients

- 1/3 cup caster sugar
- 4 ½ cups sweet stale bread, cubed
- 1/2 tablespoon candied lemon peel
- 1/3 cup dried currants
- 2 ½ tablespoons butter
- 1/2 teaspoon vanilla essence
- A pinch of kosher salt
- 1/2 teaspoon cinnamon powder
- 2 ¼ cups milk
- 4 eggs, beaten
- 1 ½ cups heavy cream

Directions

1. Prepare your cooker by adding 3 cups of water. Add the steam rack, too.
2. Take a casserole dish that will fit in the inner pot. Then, butter the casserole dish. Add bread cubes to the dish.
3. Combine the remaining ingredients in a mixing bowl; whisk vigorously until everything is well combined. Pour the mixture over the bread cubes. Next, cover with two layers of foil.
4. Select the "Steam" function and cook for 14 minutes or until the pudding is set. Remove the casserole dish from the cooker. Serve.

– DESSERTS –

142. Vegan Pumpkin Cake

Here is a dairy-free and egg-free recipe that is actually lip-smacking good! If you're going vegan or you have an allergy, give this recipe a try!

Servings 10

Ready in about 35 minutes

NUTRITIONAL INFORMATION
(Per Serving)

207 - Calories
0.4g - Fat
49.5g - Carbs
3.0g - Protein
28.6g - Sugars

Ingredients
- 1 ¼ cups pumpkin puree
- 1 cup applesauce
- 1 ¼ cups sugar
- A pinch of salt
- 2 cups flour
- 1 teaspoon ginger, grated
- 1/2 teaspoon vanilla extract
- 1 ½ teaspoons baking soda
- 1/2 teaspoon pumpkin pie spice

Directions
1. In a mixing bowl, combine the flour, vanilla extract, baking soda, pumpkin pie spice, and the salt.
2. In a separate bowl, combine the applesauce and the sugar. Stir in the ginger and the pumpkin puree and mix well to combine.
3. Add the applesauce mixture to the dry flour mixture. Spoon batter into a cake pan oiled with cooking spray. Cover with a foil.
4. Pour 2 cups of water into the cooker. Lay a metal rack on the bottom of your cooker. Lay prepared cake pan on the metal rack. Cook for 24 minutes at HIGH pressure.
5. Transfer the pan to a wire rack before serving. Dust your cake with icing sugar or decorate with vegan frosting. Enjoy!

– DESSERTS –

143. Pumpkin Chocolate Bundt Cake

Add a festive look to your dessert table every day with this appetizing cake. You can add colored sanding sugars for even prettier presentation!

Servings 10

Ready in about 25 minutes

NUTRITIONAL INFORMATION
(Per Serving)

430 - Calories
20.6g - Fat
57.1g - Carbs
6.3g - Protein
34.9g - Sugars

Ingredients

- 1 ¼ cups pumpkin puree
- 1 teaspoon ginger, grated
- 1 ½ sticks butter, room temperature
- 1/4 teaspoon grated nutmeg
- 1/2 teaspoon ground cinnamon
- 1/2 teaspoon ground cloves
- 1 teaspoon baking soda
- 1/2 teaspoon baking powder
- 2 cups all-purpose flour
- 1/4 teaspoon salt
- 3 large eggs
- 1 ¼ cups sugar
- 1 cup chocolate chips

Directions

1. In a bowl, mix the flour, baking soda, baking powder, nutmeg, cloves, cinnamon, and salt. Now, set it aside.
2. Then, cream the butter together with sugar using an electric mixer. Then, fold in the eggs (one at a time). Stir in the ginger and pumpkin; mix until everything is well blended.
3. Combine the reserved dry mixture with the butter mixture. Lastly, add the chocolate chips and stir to combine.
4. Spoon batter into a half-sized Bundt pan greased with non-stick cooking spray. Cover with an aluminum foil.
5. Next, prepare your Instant Pot by adding 1 ½ cups of water. Then, place the rack on the bottom. Lay the Bundt pan on the rack. Cook at HIGH pressure for 25 minutes.
6. Place your cake on a wire rack to cool before slicing and serving. Enjoy!

– DESSERTS –

144. Tropical Tapioca Pudding

Tapioca is high in iron and carbohydrates but low in fat. This delectable and aromatic dessert evokes childhood memories and brings a family together.

Servings 4

Ready in about 10 minutes

NUTRITIONAL INFORMATION
(Per Serving)

251 - Calories
4.6g - Fat
49.4g - Carbs
5.0g - Protein
31.7g - Sugars

Ingredients

- 1 ¼ cups pineapple, diced
- 3/4 cup nectarine, diced
- 2 ¼ cups whole milk
- 1/2 teaspoon vanilla paste
- 1/2 teaspoon cardamom
- 1/2 teaspoon lemon zest, grated
- 1/3 cup sugar
- 1/2 cup small pearl tapioca, soaked

Directions

1. Prepare your Instant Pot by adding 1½ cups of water; then, insert the rack and set aside.
2. Rinse tapioca and add it to a heat-proof bowl. Add the milk, sugar, lemon zest, cardamom, and vanilla paste. Add the bowl to the cooker.
3. Cover and choose "Manual" setting; cook for 9 minutes under HIGH pressure.
4. While your tapioca pudding is still warm, add the fruits. Gently stir to combine and serve at room temperature.

– DESSERTS –

145. Star Anise Chocolate Cake

Inspired by black chocolate, you can come up with this dessert idea that's so easy and literally scrumptious! This recipe calls for fresh grated ginger; you can substitute it for a crystalized ginger.

Servings 10

Ready in about 12 minutes

NUTRITIONAL INFORMATION
(Per Serving)

323 - Calories
18.1g - Fat
37.3g - Carbs
4.1g - Protein
33.2g - Sugars

Ingredients

- 3 eggs
- 1/4 cup flour
- 1/2 teaspoon grated nutmeg
- 1/2 teaspoon grated ginger
- 1 teaspoon anise seeds
- 1 cup sugar
- 1 stick butter
- 1 ½ cups black chocolate chips
- Icing sugar, for garnish

Directions

1. Microwave the chocolate chips and butter until they are completely melted or about 1 minute. Add sugar, anise seeds, ginger, nutmeg, flour and eggs.
2. Beat for 5 minutes, until everything is well mixed or until there are no lumps.
3. Pour the batter into a buttered cake pan. Insert the trivet into your Instant Pot. Pour in 3 cups of water. Place the cake pan on the trivet.
4. Cook for 7 minutes on "Manual" mode. Afterwards, perform the quick release. Let it cool completely. After that, invert the cake onto a serving platter and dust it with icing sugar. Enjoy!

– DESSERTS –

146. Banana-Vanilla Rice Pudding

When you are in a hurry or you're just not in the mood to cook, it's good to have this recipe on hand. Everyone can throw the ingredients into the pot and set the timer, right?!

Servings 6

Ready in about 22 minutes

NUTRITIONAL INFORMATION
(Per Serving)

335 - Calories
1.3g - Fat
77.5g - Carbs
4.1g - Protein
24.0g - Sugars

Ingredients

- 3 large-sized ripe bananas, divided
- 2 ½ cups vanilla rice milk
- 1 ½ cups basmati rice
- 1/2 teaspoon vanilla extract
- 1/8 teaspoon kosher salt
- 1/2 cup sugar
- 1 ½ cups water
- Ground cardamom, for garnish

Directions

1. Add the rice, water, vanilla rice milk, sugar, and salt to your Instant Pot.
2. Push the "Manual" button and cook for 11 minutes. Afterwards, remove the cooker's lid.
3. Let the pudding rest for 6 to 8 minutes before releasing pressure. Add vanilla extract and 2 mashed bananas. Stir to combine. Cut the remaining banana into thin slices.
4. Divide the pudding among the serving bowls; serve topped with banana slices and ground cardamom. Enjoy!

– DESSERTS –

147. Cheesecake with Cranberry Topping

No more excuses for not making desserts! Even the cheesecake with a special holiday flavor! This cheesecake has a mild flavor and flaky crust, so it pairs perfectly with fresh cranberries.

Servings 12

Ready in about 42 minutes + chilling time

NUTRITIONAL INFORMATION (Per Serving)

330 - Calories
23.8g - Fat
25.5g - Carbs
4.8g - Protein
18.8g - Sugars

Ingredients

For the Cake:
- 3 whole eggs
- 3/4 tablespoon flour
- 1 stick butter, melted
- 1 ¾ cups cream cheese, softened
- 1/2 teaspoon anise seed
- 1/4 teaspoon cinnamon powder
- 1/3 cup sugar
- 1/3 cup sour cream
- 1 1/3 cups biscuits, roughly broken

For the Topping:
- 3/4 cup golden caster sugar
- 1 1/3 cups cranberries
- 2 teaspoons ground arrowroot
- Cold water

Directions

1. In a bowl, combine the butter with biscuits. Spread the mixture around the bottom of a lightly springform pan.
2. Next, beat the sugar and cream cheese with an electric mixer. Add the sour cream, cinnamon, anise seed, and flour. Fold in the eggs, one at a time; continue mixing until it is creamy. Pour the mixture onto the prepared crust.
3. Add 3 cups of water to the cooker. Lay the rack on the bottom. Then, lower the pan onto the rack.
4. Cover the cooker with the lid and choose the "Manual" mode. Set the timer for 35 minutes. Refrigerate your dessert overnight.
5. Meanwhile, you can make the compote; place the cranberries, sugar, and 1 cup of water in a saucepan; then, bring to a simmer for 5 minutes, stirring periodically.
6. Then, mix the arrowroot with 2 tablespoons of cold water; add the mixture to the saucepan. Cook for 2 more minutes, stirring regularly. Allow the topping to cool completely.
7. Spread the topping over your cheesecake and serve chilled.

— DESSERTS —

148. Rustic Apple Compote

When you're looking for just the right thing to serve in the late afternoon in autumn, give this recipe a try. You can use whole cloves instead of ground ones, and add a couple of prunes if desired. Serve with a large scoop of vanilla ice cream and ginger biscuits. Lovely!

Servings 8

Ready in about 7 minutes

NUTRITIONAL INFORMATION
(Per Serving)

142 - Calories
0.4g - Fat
34.8g - Carbs
0.6g - Protein
32.5g - Sugars

Ingredients

- 1 cup sugar
- 2 tablespoons brandy
- 1/4 teaspoon salt
- 1 teaspoon cloves
- 8 dried apricots, halved
- 1 ½ pounds apples, cored and diced
- 2 vanilla bean, split in half
- 2 cinnamon sticks

Directions

1. Put all of the above ingredients into a steel bowl.
2. Set a metal rack in the bottom of the Instant Pot. Place the steel bowl on the metal rack.
3. Choose the "Steam" button and cook for 7 minutes under HIGH pressure. Then, use the steam release.
4. Serve warm or at room temperature, sprinkled with chopped pecans if desired.

– DESSERTS –

149. Festive Dessert with Prunes and Pecans

Pecans are a powerhouse of vitamin E, several important B-complex groups of vitamins, minerals, beta-carotene, and lutein. Here's just one of many amazing recipes that include this superfood.

Servings 8

Ready in about 55 minutes

NUTRITIONAL INFORMATION (Per Serving)

431 - Calories
25.5g - Fat
61.1g - Carbs
6.8g - Protein
39.6g - Sugars

Ingredients

- 1 cup prunes, chopped
- 1/2 teaspoon ground ginger
- 1 ¼ cups sugar
- 2 tablespoons orange liqueur
- 4 whole eggs
- 1 ½ sticks butter
- 2 teaspoons orange zest
- 1/8 teaspoon salt
- 1/3 cup pecans, chopped
- 1 teaspoons baking powder
- 1 ¼ cups self-rising flour
- 1/2 cup double cream, for garnish

Directions

1. Firstly, beat together the butter and sugar in a dessert bowl. Add the sifted flour and baking powder. Now, whisk the eggs vigorously. Add the whisked eggs to the mixing bowl.
2. Stir in the ground ginger, salt, and orange zest. Next, add the prunes, pecans, and orange liqueur.
3. Add 3 cups of water to the Instant Pot's inner pot. Place a rack inside, and place the dessert bowl on top.
4. Select "Manual" function, HIGH pressure, and 55-minute cook time. Meanwhile, whisk the double cream.
5. Press the "Cancel" button; check for the doneness of your dessert. Decorate the pudding with cream and serve.

– DESSERTS –

150. Frozen Lime Cheesecake

In this gorgeous recipe, a good replacement for digestive biscuits would be ginger biscuits and even ginger nuts. Take your parties to a whole new level!

Servings 10

Ready in about 32 minutes + chilling time

NUTRITIONAL INFORMATION (Per Serving)

480 - Calories
37.1g - Fat
17.8g - Carbs
19.9g - Protein
10.8g - Sugars

Ingredients

- 1 teaspoon vanilla extract
- 3 tablespoons flour
- 1 teaspoon anise seeds
- 1 teaspoon grated ginger
- 2 tablespoons lemon zest, finely grated
- 2 tablespoons lime zest
- 1 stick butter, at room temperature
- 3 whole eggs, room temperature
- 1/2 cup sour cream
- 1 ½ pounds full-fat cream cheese
- 1 ½ cups digestive biscuits, crumbled
- 1/2 cup caster sugar

Directions

1. In a bowl, combine the crumbled biscuits and butter. Lightly grease the inside of a springform pan with a non-stick cooking spray. Now, press the biscuit mixture into the bottom of the spring-form pan.
2. Next, add 2½ cups of water to your Instant Pot. Now, lay a trivet at the bottom of the cooker.
3. In a food processor, mix the cream cheese together with caster sugar; process until creamy and smooth. Fold in the eggs, one at a time.
4. Add the rest of the ingredients. Pulse until everything is well blended.
5. Pour the batter into the springform pan. Cook at HIGH pressure; set the timer for 26 minutes. Wrap your cheesecake in a foil and freeze overnight. Serve.

Printed in Great Britain
by Amazon